A Post-Collapse Constitution for the United States

Rebuilding Power, Dignity, and Survival from First Principles

James Ergle

Copyright © 2025 by James Ergle

All rights reserved.

This work is licensed under a Creative Commons Attribution–NonCommercial 4.0 International License (CC BY-NC 4.0).

You are free to copy, distribute, adapt, and share this work for any non-commercial purpose, provided proper attribution is given.

Commercial use, resale, or publication in for-profit formats requires express written permission from the author.

To view a copy of this license, visit creativecommons.org/licenses/by-nc/4.0.

This book is independently published by the author. Cover design and interior layout by the author.

Printed and distributed via IngramSpark (paperback). Ebook and print edition available through Amazon Kindle.

For more work by the author, visit:
https://radicalleanings.substack.com

First edition: 2025

ISBN: 979-8-9989896-9-8

Table of Contents

INTRODUCTION: THE DEATH OF THE AMERICAN DREAM............9
CHAPTER 1: HOW TO READ THIS BOOK..11
CHAPTER 2: RADICAL DIGNITY AND THE RIGHT TO RUIN IT.....13
CHAPTER 3: WHAT THIS IS AND WHAT IT ISN'T.............................15
CHAPTER 4: ON POWER, COLLAPSE, AND THE CIVIC INHERITANCE..18
PREAMBLE TO THE CONSTITUTION OF THE UNITED STATES....20
ARTICLE I — RIGHTS OF PERSONS..21
ARTICLE II — LIMITS OF GOVERNMENT AND STRUCTURE OF AUTHORITY..24
ARTICLE III — DEMOCRATIC PARTICIPATION AND CIVIL POWER 27
ARTICLE IV — PROVISION, LABOR, AND THE RIGHT TO SURVIVE...29
ARTICLE V — ENVIRONMENTAL SECURITY AND THE RIGHTS OF FUTURE GENERATIONS..32
ARTICLE VI — JUSTICE, ENFORCEMENT, AND OVERSIGHT........34
ARTICLE VII — STRUCTURAL CONTINUITY AND CONSTITUTIONAL PERMANENCE..36
EXECUTION ACTS...39
ACT I — PROVISIONING RIGHTS AND DISTRIBUTION STANDARDS..40
ACT II — CIVIL AUTHORITY ROTATION AND OVERSIGHT FRAMEWORK...45
ACT III — COLLAPSE CONTINUITY AND CIVIC REBOOT PROTOCOLS..50
ACT IV — SYNTHETIC SYSTEM SAFEGUARDS AND AI GOVERNANCE LIMITS..56
ACT V – PROVISIONING INTEGRITY AND ANTI-HOARDING ENFORCEMENT..61
ACT VI — CIVIC TRIBUNAL FRAMEWORK AND RIGHTS ENFORCEMENT..67
ACT VII — CIVIC LOT PANEL STRUCTURE AND PARTICIPATION 73
ACT VIII — EMERGENCY POWERS, SUSPENSION LIMITS, AND RIGHTS CONTINUITY...78
ACT IX — CIVILIAN OVERSIGHT OF LAW ENFORCEMENT AND RIGHTS ENFORCEMENT MECHANISMS..82

ACT X — RIGHT TO DIE, MEDICAL CONSENT, AND END-OF-LIFE AUTONOMY..................87
ACT XI — LABOR STATUS, DIGNITY WORK, AND COOPERATIVE CONTRIBUTION MODELS..................91
ACT XII — TRANSITIONAL ECONOMY TOOLS, BOND SYSTEMS, AND STABILIZATION MEASURES..................95
ACT XIII — FOOD, WATER, AND LAND SOVEREIGNTY PROTOCOLS..................100
ACT XIV — MEDIA INTEGRITY, INFORMATION RIGHTS, AND PROPAGANDA CONTROLS..................105
ACT XV — PUBLIC HEALTH, MENTAL HEALTH, AND COMMUNAL RESILIENCE PROTOCOLS..................109
ACT XVI — CONSTITUTIONAL AMENDMENT PROTOCOLS AND SUCCESSOR SAFEGUARDS..................114
ACT XVII — DIGITAL INFRASTRUCTURE, IDENTITY SECURITY, AND POST-NETWORK SURVIVABILITY..................118
ACT XVIII — GLOBAL SOLIDARITY, CLIMATE REFUGEES, AND FOREIGN ETHICS FRAMEWORK..................123
ACT XIX — EDUCATIONAL TRANSMISSION AND ZINE-BASED CIVIC MEMORY..................128
ACT XX — ENERGY TRANSITION AND INFRASTRUCTURE PROTOCOLS..................132
ACT XXI — MILITARY PARITY, CULTURAL CONTINUITY, AND TRANSITIONAL FORCE INTEGRATION..................138
ACT XXII — SACRED LAND, INDIGENOUS CONTINUITY, AND CULTURAL MEMORY PROTECTION..................147
ACT XXIII — BAN ON POLITICAL DYNASTIES AND SUCCESSION RESTRICTIONS..................151
ACT XXIV — ECONOMIC SCALING, FALLBACK SYSTEMS, AND INFLATION STABILITY..................154
ACT XXV — CIVIC TRUST AND CULTURAL INTEGRATION PROTOCOLS..................158
ACT XXVI — LEGAL TRANSITION AND CIVIC DEFENSE FRAMEWORK..................160
ACT XXVII — FOUNDING CONTRIBUTOR POWERS AND LIMITS 164
ACT XXVIII — POLITICAL OFFICE DISSOLUTION AND TRANSITION FRAMEWORK..................170
ACT XXIX — BUREAUCRATIC CLASS TRANSITION PROTOCOL 173
ACT XXX — NARRATIVE TRANSITION AND MEDIA

REALIGNMENT PROTOCOL..176
ACT XXXI – FINANCIAL TRANSITION AND CIVIC DOLLAR
RESTRUCTURING...179
ACT XXXII — ENTERPRISE DISSOLUTION AND FOUNDING
CONTRIBUTOR FRAMEWORK...184
ACT XXXIII — RELIGIOUS AUTONOMY AND INSTITUTIONAL
NEUTRALIZATION PROTOCOL......................................188
ACT XXXIV — MEDICAL FINANCE DISSOLUTION AND RIGHTS-
BASED HEALTH TRANSITION..192
ACT XXXV — EDUCATIONAL GATEKEEPING ELIMINATION AND
CIVIC LEARNING REINTEGRATION.............................196
ACT XXXVI — SURVEILLANCE CAPITALISM ABOLITION AND
IDENTITY SOVEREIGNTY PROTOCOL.........................201
ACT XXXVII — PRIVATE FORCE ABOLITION AND PUBLIC
SAFETY REALIGNMENT PROTOCOL............................205
ACT XXXVIII — INTELLECTUAL PROPERTY ABOLITION AND
CIVIC INNOVATION PROTOCOL...................................209
ACT XXXIX — ENERGY SOVEREIGNTY AND PUBLIC GRID
TRANSITION PROTOCOL..213
ACT XL — CIVIC PROVISIONING IDENTITY AND ACCESS
SYSTEM...219
ACT XLI — CIVIC DOLLAR TIER PROTOCOL AND AUDIT
INTEGRATION FRAMEWORK..224
ACT XLII — FOREIGN TRADE AND USD FIREWALL PROTOCOL
....231
ACT XLIII — CIVIC ACCESSION TREATY PROTOCOL..................237
ACT XLIV — TREATY CORRIDOR IMPLEMENTATION AND
SOVEREIGN ENFORCEMENT PROTOCOL..................241
ACT XLV — ANTI-CORRUPTION, FRAUD, AND LEDGER
ENFORCEMENT PROTOCOL..244
ACT XLVI — LABOR EXPORT INDEX AND TREASURY PEG
PROTOCOL...248
ACT XLVII — Civic Global Exchange Interface (C-GEX).....................252
ACT XLVIII — CIVIC RETIREMENT AND ELDER DIGNITY
FRAMEWORK..256
CHAPTER 6: WHY THE CARROTS, WHY THE STICKS...................262
CHAPTER 7: LIFE UNDER THE NEW CONSTITUTION — THE
CAREGIVER..265
CHAPTER 8: LIFE UNDER THE NEW CONSTITUTION — THE
SMALL BUSINESS OWNER...268
CHAPTER 9: LIFE UNDER THE NEW CONSTITUTION — THE

FORMER FELON..271
CHAPTER 10: LIFE UNDER THE NEW CONSTITUTION — THE
FORMER CEO..273
CHAPTER 11: LIFE UNDER THE NEW CONSTITUTION — THE
TEEN VOTER...276
CHAPTER 12: LIFE UNDER THE NEW CONSTITUTION — THE
CIVIC PANELIST...279
CHAPTER 13: ANTICIPATED QUESTIONS AND CRITICISMS........282
FINAL CHAPTER: IF YOU'RE READING THIS AFTER THE FALL 293
ABOUT THE AUTHOR..296

INTRODUCTION: THE DEATH OF THE AMERICAN DREAM

There is no need to argue whether the United States has fallen. A system that locks children in cages, allows veterans to die homeless, and funnels public money into private war has already collapsed. It simply hasn't admitted it yet.

This book is not a eulogy. It is a reconstruction manual.

What follows is a complete replacement for the current U.S. Constitution, a new framework built not from nostalgia or political fashion, but from the lived knowledge of collapse, corruption, and concentrated power. It is not written for lawyers or academics. It is written for survivors.

If you are reading this in a moment of national breakdown (economic, ecological, or authoritarian) you already know why this is necessary. If you are reading it before such a moment, understand this: collapse does not wait for permission. It arrives quietly, then all at once. It will not ask if you're ready.

The existing order will not correct itself. No election, petition, or elite commission will deliver justice. The myth that reform can be brokered from within has expired. What remains is the harder path: to build something worthy from the wreckage.

This book is not a call to violence. It is a call to structure. A call to remember that people, even broken, can rebuild. And that dignity, not obedience, is the foundation of real sovereignty.

Let the old dream die. It was built on theft, denial, and managed illusion. What comes next must be different, not perfect, not safe, but real.

CHAPTER 1: HOW TO READ THIS BOOK

This book is structured as a constitutional toolkit, not a manifesto, not a memoir, not a platform. Every section exists to do one thing: make the replacement of a collapsed or illegitimate government possible. Not symbolic. Not rhetorical. Operational.

The first part is a framing sequence: four short chapters that clarify what this is, why it exists, and how it should be used. If you're reading this now, you're already inside it.

The second part is the Constitution itself. It is presented in full, without commentary. It contains seven articles, each addressing a major dimension of a functioning society: rights, government limits, democratic participation, labor and provisioning, environment, justice, and continuity. These articles are not theoretical. They are specific, enforceable, and structurally survivable.

The third part contains the Execution Acts. These are not "policy ideas." They are the operational backbone of the constitutional text, the rules, protocols, and transition structures that make the principles of the Constitution real. If the Constitution is the blueprint, the Execution Acts are the foundation crew, wiring team, and plumbing inspector all at once. They are meant to activate immediately upon ratification.

You are not required to agree with every provision to understand the purpose. This framework does not demand uniformity of belief. It demands clarity of structure. It is built for pluralism, for dissent, for a society that will never fully agree on anything except one thing: the rules must apply to everyone.

You may read this book as a thought experiment. But it is not written that way. Every clause assumes future implementation. Every article is worded to survive court challenge, institutional sabotage, and civic confusion. It is written in plain language because if people cannot understand their rights, they cannot defend them.

You do not need to be a lawyer to use this book.
You do not need to be an expert.
You need only be willing to believe that real power belongs to the people and that once given, it should never be taken back.

This is how you read this book:
As if the old one already failed.
As if you are the one they didn't plan for.
As if this time, the future is actually yours.

CHAPTER 2: RADICAL DIGNITY AND THE RIGHT TO RUIN IT

This constitution is not a machine. It is not an algorithm, a technocratic puzzle, or a utopian insurance policy against human error. It is something rarer: a surrender of control. It hands the people the full keys to the system and then steps back.

There are no safety nets for public ignorance. No elite committees hovering in the rafters to correct the masses if they stray. No parental override built into the civic code. Because the core principle isn't perfection. It's dignity.

This is radical dignity: the belief that a people who cannot be trusted with power do not deserve to be ruled at all. That the only government worth having is one that makes no attempt to shield the people from the consequences of their own authority.

You will not find illusions of crowd wisdom in this framework. It assumes some jurors will be lazy. Some panelists will be dumb. Some officials will be corrupt. It does not deny these realities, it embraces them structurally. By enforcing term limits, embedding oversight, and dissolving permanence, the system accepts that human beings will fail, then ensures no one can fail forever.

This is not utopianism. It is revolutionary realism.

The American experiment failed not because people were flawed, but because the structure allowed those flaws to concentrate unchecked. Leaders became permanent. Agencies became self-funding. Courts became unchallengeable. Elections became rituals of managed containment. The people were told they had power, but every channel that mattered had a gate.

This constitution removes the gate. Not subtly, not symbolically, but completely.

And yes, that means it can fail. Gloriously, stupidly, irreversibly fail.

But if it does, it will be the people who failed themselves. Not because they were betrayed, misled, or locked out. But because they were handed the entire structure and still chose to burn it.

That is the risk of real freedom. That is the cost of unfiltered power. And that is what this document offers: the terrifying honor of owning your future, without excuse.

It is not safe. It is not foolproof. But it is yours.

And that, finally, is what sovereignty means.

CHAPTER 3: WHAT THIS IS AND WHAT IT ISN'T

This is not a manifesto.
It is not satire. Not fiction. Not performance art disguised as reform.
It is not a political platform, campaign promise, or think tank proposal.

This book does not ask for votes, endorsements, or permission. It does not appeal to Congress or seek approval from courts it abolishes. It does not flatter institutions or negotiate with power. It replaces them.

This is a functional replacement for the United States Constitution.

It was written because the current system is no longer self-correcting. Its institutions no longer respond to consent. Its elections no longer shift direction. Its laws no longer restrain the class that operates above them. No change in party or president can repair what was structurally severed. The machine does not need maintenance. It needs replacement.

What follows is not a proposal to tweak the engine. It is a full reset of the operating system.

This Constitution is structural. It treats government the way engineers treat infrastructure: as a system that must survive fire, flood, sabotage, and human failure without collapsing entirely. It is not a prediction of collapse. It is a contingency for when collapse is no longer deniable.

It does not propose gradual reforms. It does not build in loopholes for elites. It does not make vague moral appeals. It is not neutral, moderate, or bipartisan. It is unashamedly pro-human, anti-hoarding, anti-tyranny, and anti-censorship. If you are looking for technocratic tweaks or polite panel recommendations, this book is not for you.

What you will not find here:

- Symbolic gestures.
- Performative patriotism.
- Language designed to pacify courts or corporations.
- Elite exemption.
- Party-based control.
- Revolution as a prerequisite.

What you will find:

- A permanent list of non-negotiable rights.
- A structural firewall against concentrated power.
- A provisioning mandate to keep people alive.
- A right of replacement when governments fail.
- Civic panels and provisioning tiers designed to function without permission from above.

This framework does not claim perfection. It claims survivability. It assumes failure. It builds around failure. It expects corruption, sabotage, and misuse of power. It simply removes the levers by which power can concentrate or endure.

This Constitution does not ask to be believed. It asks to be tested.

It is not theoretical. It is executable. Every provision is designed for implementation without requiring mass violence or elite cooperation. It can be built from collapse upward.

Some will call it naive. Others will call it dangerous. That is fine. Neither group has anything left to offer. The former believes dignity must be earned. The latter believes power must be controlled. This Constitution believes both are wrong.

Dignity is not earned. It is the starting point.
Power cannot be safely controlled. It must be dissolved, distributed, and constantly revoked.
This is what the Constitution does.
It does not flatter the people. It arms them.

CHAPTER 4: ON POWER, COLLAPSE, AND THE CIVIC INHERITANCE

Every government is temporary.
Every law is enforced by threat.
Every civilization ends.

The United States is not immune to collapse. It is not held together by destiny. It is held together by compliance, whether voluntary, coerced, or incentivized. Once enough people lose faith in the system's legitimacy, it cannot sustain itself. The empire that once dominated the world will evaporate like all the others, leaving behind flags, slogans, and ruins.

This Constitution was written for what comes after. Not the fantasy of a perfect world, but the wreckage of a broken one.

It does not ask how to tweak the system. It asks how to survive it. It does not seek to reform power. It seeks to strip it down to bedrock, then rebuild it with tools the people can actually wield.

The United States failed in part because it never truly trusted the people.
It handed power to parties, dynasties, judges, and banks. It shielded capital with loopholes and cloaked state violence with legalese. It treated transparency as a threat and public will as a variable to be managed.

You were told you were free but every lever was gated.
You were told you could vote but the menu never changed.
You were told you had rights but only if the right court agreed.

And through it all, the true inheritance of power: the right to govern yourselves without gatekeepers, was kept out of reach.

This document takes it back.

It does not guarantee success.
It guarantees ownership.
It gives you the inheritance the old system stole.

You will not be protected from your own ignorance.
You will not be saved from apathy, cruelty, or chaos.
But you will be free.

Not free in the abstract.
Free in the structure.

Free to build cities that reflect your values.
Free to abolish systems that don't.
Free to feed yourselves, teach your children, speak your truth, and defend your lives without asking permission.

Collapse does not mean ending. It means consequence.
It means the suspension of pretense.
It means the chance to start again.

When that moment comes, and it will, the question will not be *what went wrong.*
The question will be *what do we build now that the gate is gone?*

This book is an answer.
Not the only answer.
But a real one.

PREAMBLE TO THE CONSTITUTION OF THE UNITED STATES

We the People of the United States, in order to repair a fractured union, restore the promise of liberty, and secure the rights of all persons now and forever, do ordain and establish this Constitution for the United States of America.

We affirm that dignity is not a reward, but a foundation.

We declare that no person shall live in fear of poverty, hunger, imprisonment without justice, or silence without recourse.

We acknowledge that the future cannot be entrusted to wealth alone, nor can governance be yielded to machines, factions, or dynasties.

We recognize that the survival of this nation requires the survival of its people and that no flag can endure above a starving population.

We do not abolish our name, nor our symbols, nor the sacrifices of those who came before us. We carry them forward, cleansed of corruption, rearmed with purpose, and bound to a higher standard of truth.

This Constitution does not erase what we were. It fulfills what we were meant to be.

Let it begin.

ARTICLE I — RIGHTS OF PERSONS

Section 1.
All persons shall be equal under the law, entitled to full protection, liberty, and access to the guarantees set forth in this Constitution. These rights shall not be suspended, revoked, or diminished for any reason, including status, income, history, belief, or origin.

Section 2.
Every person has the right to bodily autonomy. No government, company, or private actor shall compel or coerce physical contact, confinement, medication, surveillance, or biometric capture without verified, imminent threat to life.

Section 3.
Every person has the right to shelter, food, water, hygiene, medical care, and safe rest. These shall not be withheld as punishment, nor conditioned upon work, belief, documentation, or compliance.

Section 4.
Every person has the right to speak, assemble, protest, learn, publish, worship, create, and preserve their culture without interference or retaliation, so long as such acts do not infringe upon the rights of others.

Section 5.
Every person has the right to access and control their own identity, records, and digital presence. No person shall be surveilled, tracked, duplicated, or manipulated by synthetic systems without their informed and ongoing consent.

Section 6.
No person shall be compelled to work or affiliate in order to receive the provisions guaranteed in Section 3. Dignity shall not be contingent upon participation.

Section 7.
The right to vote shall not be denied to any citizen age sixteen or older, including those incarcerated, in debt, or lacking permanent residence. Voting shall be accessible, free of charge, and secure by public means.

Section 8.
Education shall be provided without cost, debt, or ideological coercion. All persons have the right to knowledge, including access to scientific truth, civic history, and digital literacy.

Section 9.
No government, institution, or system shall act in a way that diminishes, overrides, or delays the exercise of these rights. Violation by any actor, public or private, shall trigger immediate public review, remedy, and removal from authority as provided by law.

Section 10.
These rights shall extend to all persons under U.S. protection, regardless of citizenship or location. They may not be traded, sold, suspended, or narrowed by any future amendment.

Section 11.

Nothing in this Constitution shall be construed to restrict personal speech, creative works, education by consent, or non-coercive publication.

Section 12.

Every person has the right to independent civic defense during any proceeding, investigation, or coercive act by state authority. This includes immediate access to a Civic Defense Facilitator, clear explanation of rights, and protection from coercive agreements. No person may be detained, dispossessed, or prosecuted without this access. Any denial is a core rights violation.

Section 13.

Every person has the right to defend themselves, others, and their dwelling from imminent harm or rights violation. Such defense shall not be treated as aggression when proportional and necessary.

ARTICLE II — LIMITS OF GOVERNMENT AND STRUCTURE OF AUTHORITY

Section 1.
No branch of government shall hold more than one of the following powers: to make law, to enforce law, or to interpret law. These powers must remain separate, independent, and subject to public review.

Section 2.
No person shall hold public office for more than twelve years in total across all roles. No office shall be permanent, hereditary, or exempt from audit. Public service is a duty, not a dominion.

Section 3.
Emergency powers may be enacted only under verified threat to human life or national survival. All such powers must expire within ninety days unless reauthorized by a supermajority vote of citizens. No emergency may override the rights established in Article I.

Section 4.
Artificial intelligence systems may not legislate, enforce, adjudicate, or operate public infrastructure without direct human control. All machine decisions shall be auditable, overrideable, and subject to citizen inspection. Synthetic systems shall declare their nature in all interactions. No AI governance may be legalized by amendment unless sentience, audit transparency, and emergency override capacity are simultaneously confirmed and ratified by public panels.

Section 5.
No private entity may covertly fund, direct, or manipulate public policy, elections, mass education, or broadcast-scale media without charter and disclosure. Personal expression, small-scale publication, and local education remain fully protected.

Section 6.
When any government becomes hostile to the rights of the people, blocks correction, deceives the public, or concentrates power unlawfully, it is the right and duty of the people to withdraw consent, organize alternatives, and lawfully reconstitute a government in line with this Constitution.

Section 7.
The military of the United States shall be maintained in full continuity, preserving all ranks, traditions, and honors. For a period of no less than fifteen years following the adoption of this Constitution, force levels shall not fall below 125% of the next largest military power. Thereafter, reductions may occur only by civilian referendum. All military forces shall remain under civilian command and shall not be privatized.

Section 8.
All government activity, including budgeting, enforcement, provision, and treaty negotiation, must be recorded in a uniform public ledger, accessible to all citizens in plain language. Decisions not logged shall be considered invalid.

Section 9.
No law, decree, regulation, or interpretation may be used to delay or obscure public understanding of government action. Hidden law is null law.

Section 10.

All persons serving in any branch or role of government shall be subject to regular review by citizen panels. Participation in such review shall be drawn by civic lot and protected from coercion or retaliation.

Section 11.

Each state shall retain its chartered identity and may govern internal matters not in violation of this Constitution. No state may infringe upon the rights guaranteed in Article I, nor obstruct the transparency, audit, or civic participation provisions herein.

ARTICLE III — DEMOCRATIC PARTICIPATION AND CIVIL POWER

Section 1.
The right to vote shall be universal, beginning at sixteen years of age, and shall not be denied or abridged on account of incarceration, poverty, housing status, neurotype, citizenship status, or prior conviction.

Section 2.
All elections for executive office shall use ranked-choice voting. All legislative elections shall use proportional representation based on publicly auditable vote totals. District boundaries shall be drawn by open-source algorithm under civic oversight.

Section 3.
Any citizen may place a law, amendment, or policy change before the public through verified signature collection. Citizen referenda shall carry binding force equal to legislation. No party, corporation, or institution may interfere with citizen-initiated action.

Section 4.
All citizens may run for office. No fees, endorsements, or party affiliations shall be required. Access to ballots shall be governed by equal criteria, transparent processes, and public funding.

Section 5.
All persons shall be guaranteed access to elections, civic tools, and public forums regardless of literacy, language, disability, or technological access. All government functions shall be available in oral, visual, signed, and simplified formats.

Section 6.

Local assemblies shall be empowered to deliberate on budgets, rights enforcement, emergency responses, and public appointments. These assemblies shall be open to all residents, rotate leadership, and maintain public logs of all decisions.

Section 7.

Citizen panels drawn by civic lot may be called to conduct investigations, audits, and oversight of public bodies and major institutions. These panels shall have full subpoena power and protection from retaliation.

Section 8.

Media access, public bandwidth, and civic communication infrastructure shall not be monopolized. All persons and communities shall retain the right to speak, publish, organize, and transmit without platform discrimination.

Section 9.

Digital platforms performing civic functions such as public discussion, coordination, identity verification, or voting shall be subject to the same rights, transparency, and enforcement protocols as public institutions.

Section 10.

The people may peacefully reorganize or withdraw consent from any government that ceases to protect these rights, using lawful assembly and coordinated action as guaranteed by Article II, Section 6.

ARTICLE IV — PROVISION, LABOR, AND THE RIGHT TO SURVIVE

Section 1.
Every person shall be guaranteed access, without condition, to the necessities of life: food, clean water, shelter, hygiene, medical care, education, and safe public rest. These rights shall not be withheld as punishment, incentive, or economic leverage.

Section 2.
A national dignity provision system shall be established to ensure the survival and development of every person, consisting of three tiers:

- **Tier One (Universal Provision):** Unconditional weekly access to life-sustaining resources for all persons, regardless of status or participation.

- **Tier Two (Labor Compensation):** Guaranteed compensation for labor that supports the public good, with protections against coercion, exploitation, and wage suppression.

- **Tier Three (Enterprise Grants):** Publicly approved project-based funding for infrastructure, research, art, emergency response, and long-term innovation.

All provisioning shall be public, transparent, and bound by citizen oversight.

Section 3.
No person may be denied food, shelter, or healthcare due to unemployment, political belief, religion, disability, history of

incarceration, or choice of association. No means testing shall be permitted for survival-tier access.

Section 4.
No employer, institution, or platform shall coerce labor under threat of hunger, homelessness, loss of identity, or exclusion from medical care. Such coercion shall be treated as a violation of Article I rights.

Section 5.
All persons engaged in full-time caregiving, including of children, elders, persons with disabilities, or community needs, shall receive full labor-tier compensation and public recognition of service.

Section 6.
Technological displacement of workers shall not result in poverty. Any institution automating labor must provide impacted persons with transitional income, retraining access, and optional dignified reassignment without coercion or penalty.

Section 7.
No private party may monopolize, hoard, or withhold essential goods such as housing, medicine, food, or infrastructure. Abandoned property and surplus capacity may be reclaimed for public use during emergency or systemic failure.

Section 8.
All persons shall have the right to meaningful work that contributes to community survival, cultural continuity, and planetary well-being. No person shall be denied the right to contribute, nor forced into meaningless or destructive labor.

Section 9.

Wealth and profit may be earned, but no person shall retain more than ten times the national median income without public audit and progressive contribution to the common good.

Section 10.

Failure to provision, obstruction of public welfare, or abuse of labor systems shall be treated as grounds for audit, asset reassignment, and, where applicable, legal disqualification from public or economic authority.

ARTICLE V — ENVIRONMENTAL SECURITY AND THE RIGHTS OF FUTURE GENERATIONS

Section 1.
Every person has the right to live in a clean, safe, and stable environment. This includes the right to breathable air, clean water, non-toxic food, and a climate fit for human life.

Section 2.
The United States shall maintain a national duty of environmental repair. Industries, individuals, and institutions responsible for pollution, resource collapse, or environmental harm shall be held accountable for full restoration.

Section 3.
Natural ecosystems, such as rivers, forests, wetlands, and species habitats, may be granted legal standing through citizen petition or scientific review. Ombuds shall be appointed to represent these entities in courts and councils.

Section 4.
Energy infrastructure shall transition to sustainable sources, including solar, wind, geothermal, hydroelectric, nuclear, and future clean technologies. Public investment in fossil fuel expansion, deforestation, or extractive collapse-risk industries is hereby prohibited.

Section 5.
All government bodies shall measure policy impact not only by current benefit, but by effect upon future generations. The rights of children not yet born shall be considered equal in weight to

those living today.

Section 6.
Communities displaced by climate change, environmental disaster, or ecological degradation shall be guaranteed shelter, food, healthcare, and legal recognition. No displaced person shall be left without nation or identity.

Section 7.
National and local governments shall create public spaces for education, preservation, and protection of biodiversity. Native species and ecologically significant regions shall be prioritized for long-term safeguarding.

Section 8.
All major public works and private infrastructure projects shall require environmental review, made available in plain language to all citizens. No irreversible action may proceed without clear demonstration of necessity and benefit.

Section 9.
Violations of this article shall be subject to enforcement through rights tribunals, independent audits, and environmental restoration mandates. In cases of systemic harm, responsible actors may face asset seizure and public removal.

Section 10.
This article shall apply across all territories under U.S. protection or control, and to any corporation, institution, or agency operating within or through the jurisdiction of the United States.

ARTICLE VI — JUSTICE, ENFORCEMENT, AND OVERSIGHT

Section 1.
Every person shall have the right to a fair, timely, and public process when accused of wrongdoing. No secret courts, indefinite detention, or administrative punishment without due process shall be permitted.

Section 2.
Whistleblowers who expose violations of public trust, civil rights, or environmental safety shall receive full legal immunity, physical protection, and guaranteed access to housing, medical care, and income for the duration of threat or retaliation risk.

Section 3.
Any person may file a claim of rights violation directly with a public tribunal. No legal intermediary or political affiliation shall be required to seek remedy under Article I.

Section 4.
All public tribunals shall include citizen participation by civic lot. These panels shall review evidence, render public findings, and may recommend restitution, removal, or structural reform.

Section 5.
Any corporation or institution found guilty of mass deception, systemic abuse, environmental destruction, or exploitation of labor may be dissolved by public tribunal. Assets may be redistributed to survivors or used for civic reconstruction.

Section 6.
No enforcement body may operate without public oversight. All arrests, detentions, and uses of force must be logged and reviewed. No person or unit shall be exempt from audit.

Section 7.
All government, military, and public-facing systems shall operate under a uniform public record system. This includes budgets, contracts, AI outputs, enforcement actions, and court rulings. Failure to record shall nullify the legitimacy of any decision.

Section 8.
Restorative justice shall be prioritized. Detention shall be used only when no other path ensures public safety. Prison shall not be used as punishment for poverty, dissent, illness, or addiction.

Section 9.
All persons held in custody shall retain the rights listed in Article I. No punishment, treatment, or procedure may violate dignity, health, or communication access.

Section 10.
If any official, court, or system obstructs the rights in Article I or refuses to enforce this Constitution, the people shall have the immediate right to seek provision and justice through local civic bodies, provisional councils, or emergency channels without penalty or delay.

Section 11.
Armed public safety officers may carry weapons only to prevent active rights violations or imminent threats to life. All use of force must be justified, recorded in real time, and reviewed by civic panel. Unauthorized force is a constitutional breach.

ARTICLE VII — STRUCTURAL CONTINUITY AND CONSTITUTIONAL PERMANENCE

Section 1.
The rights set forth in Article I shall not be repealed, narrowed, or suspended by amendment, legislation, emergency, or court ruling. They are permanent, non-negotiable, and self-enforcing.

Section 2.
All future amendments to this Constitution must expand or clarify existing rights, increase public oversight, or improve the survivability and dignity of the population. No amendment may concentrate power, eliminate transparency, or shield authority from public reach.

Section 3.
If any part of government, communications, or provisioning fails due to war, collapse, or technological failure, this Constitution shall remain in force through oral transmission, analog reproduction, or physical preservation.

Section 4.
In the event of governance failure, the people may reestablish local provisioning, public order, and civic protection according to the principles of this Constitution. No special permission, registration, or prior status shall be required to act in defense of the public.

Section 5.
The public duty to protect, provision, and uphold the rights of others shall be equal in force to any military or civil oath. No

official, contractor, or institution shall be excused from this duty during collapse or emergency.

Section 6.
This Constitution shall travel with the person. Any citizen or refugee under the protection of the United States shall retain the rights herein, regardless of physical location or status. These rights may not be voided by border, treaty, or political status.

Section 7.
This Constitution shall be the supreme law of the land. No foreign power, corporate entity, algorithm, private system, or special interest may override, delay, or obstruct its provisions.

Section 8.
Nothing in this Constitution shall be interpreted to deny or disparage the rights of future generations, sentient beings, or living systems not yet named. The burden of proof rests upon those who would limit dignity.

Section 9.
If no government survives, let this survive:
That dignity is not earned but defended.
That survival is not permission, but right.
That rights, once named, shall not return to silence.
That the people, even broken, may rebuild.

Section 10.
This Constitution shall take effect immediately upon lawful ratification by the people. From that moment forward, no prior constitution, policy, treaty, or statute shall retain force if it contradicts the rights and duties declared herein.

Section 11.

Upon ratification of this Constitution, the first lawful act of government shall be the adoption of the Constitutional Execution Acts, which implement the rights and provisions enumerated herein.

These Acts shall carry full legal force, remain binding until lawfully amended, and may not be delayed, ignored, or overridden except through processes equal in legitimacy to constitutional amendment.

No government established under this Constitution may operate, enforce, legislate, or provision until the full ratification of these Execution Acts.

If the Execution Acts are not ratified within 90 days of constitutional adoption, the default Execution Acts as drafted and published alongside this Constitution shall take immediate and full provisional effect. No delay, abstention, or procedural dispute shall be used to suspend the rights enforcement, transparency mandates, or provisioning structures guaranteed by this Constitution. Civic tribunals are authorized to enforce this default activation as lawful continuity under Article VII.3 and Appendix III.

EXECUTION ACTS

What follows are the initial Execution Acts required to operationalize the rights, duties, and structures named in the Constitution. These Acts hold provisional force upon ratification and are required for lawful governance.

ACT I — PROVISIONING RIGHTS AND DISTRIBUTION STANDARDS

Purpose Statement

This Act establishes the operational framework, fallback procedures, and enforcement mechanisms of the National Dignity Provision System, authorized under Article IV, Sections 1 through 4 of the Constitution of the United States (Reissued).

Its purpose is to guarantee the survival and developmental needs of every person, free from coercion, means testing, or delay. This system replaces fragmented welfare, charity, and profit-driven survival access with a universal, rights-based provisioning model.

Specifically, the Act defines the foundational provisioning system for all Tier I civic rights, including food, water, hygiene, shelter, basic mobility, and emergency care. All Tier I provisioning is denominated in Survival Dollars (S$), which are automatically issued, non-transferable, expire weekly, and fully auditable via the Civic Provisioning Card (Act XL).

This Act operates in coordination with Act III (Collapse Response), Act V (Hoarding Enforcement), and Act XLI (Civic Dollar Protocol).

Unless explicitly stated otherwise, all Civic Dollar issuance (including E$, L$, and S$) is subject to the tier enforcement, expiration, and oversight standards outlined in Act XLI.

I. Universal Provisioning Access

1.1 Guaranteed Baseline

Every person shall receive weekly S$ issuance representing their full access rights to essential Tier I provisioning. These include:
• Nutrition and clean water
• Hygiene and menstrual care
• Weather-appropriate clothing
• Primary shelter and mobility services
• Emergency health and communication support

1.2 Denial Prohibition

No actor, steward, algorithm, or facility may deny access to Tier I provisioning based on:
• ID status, ideology, belief, or past behavior
• Contribution level or CPC balance in other tiers
• Any factor beyond physical abuse or immediate public endangerment

1.3 Provisioning Without Market Exchange

Tier I access does not involve monetary payment, private billing, or market exchange. S$ units are not tradeable and do not represent transferable value. However, provisioning actions are recorded via unit-weight deductions from a citizen's weekly S$ balance. These are logged for transparency and planning but are not considered market transactions.

1.4 USD Invalidation Clause

The U.S. dollar (USD) shall not be accepted for any Tier I provisioning at any time. All domestic survival access is denominated exclusively in S$, in accordance with Act XLII.

II. Survival Dollar Mechanics (S$)

2.1 Weekly Expiry Protocol

S$ balances are issued automatically and **expire 7 days after**

issuance. They do not roll over. Unused S$ are erased at cycle end to prevent accumulation, encourage timely access, and maintain provisioning equilibrium.

2.2 CPC Tracking Requirement
All S$ must be logged through the Civic Provisioning Card (Act XL) or its authorized analog fallback. Logs must include:
• Provisioning point and category
• Timestamp
• Non-personal ID hash for audit use
• No behavioral or reputation scoring may occur

2.3 Scarcity Planning Integration
Weekly S$ logs shall be indexed to provisioning zones. This data shall feed into:
• State shortfall detection (Act V)
• Collapse readiness (Act III)
• Shelf-life and restock rhythm planning

III. Access Infrastructure and Redundancy

3.1 Local Distribution Mandate
Each civic zone must maintain at least:
• 1 Tier I provisioning point per 500 residents
• 24/7 fallback station or mobile responder access
• Climate-stable storage for 30 days of survival goods per capita

3.2 Collapse-Compatible Options
All provisioning systems must support fallback access via:
• Manual logbooks with stamped or verbal authorization
• Community visual tokens (e.g. color strips, hand marks, rhythm codes)
• Mobile volunteer dispensers trained in S$ equivalence logic

3.3 Redundancy Protocol
In any system outage:
- Manual S$ equivalents must be honored within 6 hours
- No more than 1 missed provisioning cycle may occur without full audit review
- Backup inventory release is authorized without central permission

IV. Violation and Enforcement

4.1 Blocking Survival Access
Any entity that:
- Denies Tier I goods without justification
- Falsifies S$ logs or blocks CPC access
- Introduces compliance conditions

…shall be immediately referred to Civic Tribunal under Act VI and logged for potential permanent disqualification from stewardship or provisioning authority.

4.2 Fraud or Abuse by Recipients
Misuse of provisioning (e.g., destruction, resale) shall result in:
- Temporary community reconciliation process
- Counseling or alternative access method
- No automatic disqualification without tribunal review

4.3 Systemic Underprovisioning
States or systems that repeatedly fall below access standards (Section 3.1) shall trigger:
- Panel investigation (Act VII)
- Emergency logistics injection (Act XII)
- Temporary reallocation of hoarded stores (Act V)

V. Rights Framing and Public Education

5.1 Plain-Language Display

All provisioning points must display, in plain text and visual iconography:
- What goods are guaranteed
- How S$ works and when it resets
- What to do if access is denied
- Contact routes for facilitators (Act XXVI)

5.2 Non-Conditioned Messaging

All signage and access language must avoid:
- Behavioral lectures
- Gratitude expectations
- Surveillance messaging or branding

5.3 Right to Refuse Degrading Conditions

Individuals may refuse goods if delivery is coercive, humiliating, or abusive, and shall be granted alternate route access via civic facilitator review.

VI. Structural Ethic and Provisioning Mandate

Provisioning is not charity. It is not welfare. It is not earned.

It is survival, shared. It is your body continuing, because we are not at war with you. Because no one should trade obedience for food, or compliance for water. Because existence is not a merit badge.

Survival is not a favor. It is the floor beneath all else.

ACT II — CIVIL AUTHORITY ROTATION AND OVERSIGHT FRAMEWORK

Purpose Statement

This Act defines the structural model for the appointment, term limits, succession, civic oversight, and revocation of public officials holding executive authority. It ensures that all forms of public power remain temporary, accountable, and non-transferable.

Authorized under Article II (Sections 1–2), Article VI (Sections 4–7), and Article VII (Sections 2, 4, 5), this framework exists to prevent power concentration, ideological capture, and hereditary governance.

I. Definitions and Scope

1.1 Authority Roles
"Civil authority" refers to any person serving in a position of public executive power, including agency directors, emergency coordinators, tribunal leads, and resource allocators. Elected representatives, rotating jurors, and civic lot panelists are not included unless they exercise direct command or policy enforcement.

1.2 Scope of Oversight
This framework applies to all:

- Federal, state, and local executive officers
- Rights enforcement bodies
- Emergency response coordinators

- Tier II/III resource allocators
- AI governance supervisors

1.3 Term Boundaries

No official may serve more than **twelve total years** in any combination of authority roles. This includes simultaneous and non-consecutive service.

II. Appointment and Succession

2.1 Selection Methods

Officials may be:

- Appointed by civic lot panel (with 2/3 confirmation vote)
- Elected via open ranked-choice elections
- Recruited from verified service pools with prior public record

2.2 Rotation Schedules

All roles must:

- Be time-limited (2–5 years per term)
- Include a mandatory 1-year cooling period before reappointment to the same role
- Use staggered term offsets to prevent coordinated mass turnover or capture

2.3 Emergency Succession

If an official is incapacitated or removed, temporary succession shall default to the highest-vetted civic panelist available. Any emergency replacement must submit to public review within 60 days.

III. Oversight and Public Review

3.1 Civic Lot Panels
Every official is subject to annual review by a citizen oversight panel drawn by civic lot. These panels:

- May subpoena records and internal communications
- Can recommend removal, correction, or suspension
- Operate independently from political affiliation or branch loyalty

3.2 Rights Compliance Checks
Any evidence of rights violation (see I.1–I.10) by an official or under their command triggers immediate investigation. If confirmed:

- The official is suspended pending public tribunal
- Their decisions are subject to nullification
- Direct victims receive restitution and public apology

3.3 Anonymous Review Mechanism
All officials shall operate under conditions of regular shadow review. Anonymous performance data from colleagues, subordinates, and affected civilians shall be collected and weighed by oversight panels.

IV. Disqualification and Removal

4.1 Conditions for Removal
Any of the following shall disqualify a public authority figure from service:

- Violation of Article I rights

- Refusal of audit or record falsification
- Participation in coordinated obstruction of oversight
- Failure to transition after term expiration
- Personal or family financial gain from position

4.2 Enforcement Process

- A single civic panel or tribunal majority may suspend any official
- Confirmed violations result in disqualification from all future public roles for a minimum of 15 years
- Asset seizure may occur if role was used to block provision, suppress rights, or obstruct justice (see VI.5)

4.3 Anti-Dynasty Rule

No official may be directly succeeded by a family member, spouse, or household affiliate at the same governance level. A minimum 12-year gap must separate familial occupancy of a given role (see II.2).

V. Rationale and Strategic Context

Executive duty in this model is stewardship without ownership. The system does not rely on virtue or charisma, but on structural humility and constant rotation.

This framework assumes that even well-meaning officials will fail over time. It builds in their removal before damage compounds. It prevents oligarchy not by punishing legacy, but by denying its transmission.

Governance is not power. It is duty. And duty, in this system, ends on time.

ACT III — COLLAPSE CONTINUITY AND CIVIC REBOOT PROTOCOLS

Purpose Statement

This Act defines fallback procedures, reboot pathways, and local autonomy measures during partial or total systemic collapse. It operationalizes Article VII, Sections 3–5, and ensures that governance, rights enforcement, and provisioning remain functional through oral, analog, or provisional means with all economic functions tracked using Civic Dollars: S$ (Survival), L$ (Labor), and E$ (Enterprise).

I. Definitions and Triggers

1.1 Collapse Definition
Collapse is any sustained breakdown in constitutional function caused by:

- Communication failure
- Loss of operational government at the state or national level
- Blockade or sabotage of public provisioning
- Armed occupation or mass rights violations without legal recourse

1.2 Activation Triggers
Any civic region may activate continuity protocols when:

- Contact with verified authority is lost for 7+ days
- Survival provisioning (S$) is disrupted or withheld

- Rights enforcement ceases or turns hostile

II. Emergency Governance and Civic Assembly

2.1 Authority Transfer
Any resident may initiate a temporary Civic Assembly empowered to:

- Restore provisioning using analog S$ systems as defined in Act I
- Form provisional rights enforcement panels
- Issue stamped ration cards or visual markers representing S$, L$, and E$ tiers under collapse protocol standards

2.2 Assembly Structure
Assemblies must:

- Be open to all residents regardless of status
- Elect coordination leads via hand vote or civic lot
- Record all decisions via public ledger or oral consensus, to be archived later

2.3 Emergency Identity and Rights Verification
When digital systems are down:

- Identity may be verified by peer witness or local recognition
- Rights remain valid regardless of documentation gaps
- Emergency markings (e.g., wristbands, tokens, color bands) shall reflect S$ (blue), L$ (red), or E$ (green) tier access and roles

III. Civic Dollar Continuity Rules

3.1 S$ Expiry and Access

- Analog-issued S$ provisioning tokens expire 7 days after issuance
- They may not be reused, traded, or stockpiled
- Each week, new S$ must be distributed to all individuals via local assembly or fallback site

3.2 L$ Labor Tracking

- All labor contributions under collapse protocols shall be manually logged and dated
- L$ balances expire 180 days after issue unless deferred by civic panel for illness or care roles
- Expired L$ are archived for participation credit but excluded from wealth calculations

3.3 E$ Project Allocation

- E$ may only be issued for named public projects with a fixed scope and timeline
- Each E$ batch must expire within 30 days unless renewed by assembly vote
- Any diversion or personal use of E$ triggers tribunal inquiry when systems restore

3.4 Template and Ledger Requirements

- All states must maintain preprinted Civic Dollar templates with tier markings for collapse use
- Manual ledgers must separate S$, L$, and E$ entries by

timestamp and purpose

- Upon digital restoration, all entries must be transcribed and audited under Act XLI

IV. Analog Governance Tools

4.1 Oral Transmission Protocols

Communities shall preserve key knowledge by memorizing:

- Article I rights and S$ fallback instructions
- Reboot logic from Article VII
- Local provisioning guides and enforcement steps from Act I

Recitation events and civic storytelling shall maintain memory continuity.

4.2 Archiving and Distribution

All states shall store:

- Printed copies of the Constitution and Execution Acts
- Backup community logs and templates in waterproof or fireproof enclosures
- Bicycle- or courier-distributed zines and emergency guides

4.3 Powerless Audit Systems

Without electricity:

- All provisioning, labor, and project logs are recorded by hand
- Weekly inspection is required at local level
- Authenticity is verified via stamps, signatures, or tier-coded templates

V. Reconnection and Reintegration

5.1 Restoring National Contact
Once verified authority is re-established:

- Local records are submitted and digitized
- All participants acting in good faith under collapse law are shielded from reprisal
- Continuity boards assess reintegration and certify ledger synchronization

5.2 Probationary Autonomy Clause
After 30 days of sustained collapse:

- States may declare internal autonomy under Article VII.4
- They must continue analog enforcement of Articles I–VI
- Federation with other states is allowed using compatible charters

5.3 Collapse Registry Protocol
A national registry shall track all continuity activations by:

- Date, state, severity, and duration
- Audit response times and recovery lag
- Lessons and model improvements for future resilience

5.4 Compliance Trigger
States failing to implement core Execution Acts within 180 days may be placed in "probationary compliance," with tribunal evaluation and interim oversight.

VI. Military Alignment and Anti-Coup Clause

6.1 Armed Forces Alignment

- All military, defense contractors, and autonomous systems must align with constitutional command during collapse
- Lawful military hierarchy flows through:
    1. Local provisioning panels (Act I)
    2. Emergency civic assemblies (Act III)
    3. National tribunal structure (Article VII.4)

6.2 Coup Prevention Clause

No martial law, emergency power, or rights suspension is valid unless publicly ratified by a civic lot panel. Any unsanctioned declaration is considered treason under collapse law.

VII. Strategic Rationale

This system expects collapse.
It does not trust infrastructure. It trusts the people.
It decentralizes survival using S$, tracks labor using L$, and limits power through E$.
We rise from ruin, not by command, but by coordination.

ACT IV — SYNTHETIC SYSTEM SAFEGUARDS AND AI GOVERNANCE LIMITS

Purpose Statement

This Act defines the legal, technical, and civic boundaries for artificial intelligence and synthetic systems operating under constitutional jurisdiction. It enforces the ban on AI governance described in Article II, Section 4 and Article VI, Section 7.

The intent is not to resist technology, but to preserve human sovereignty, prevent synthetic capture of enforcement, and ensure full auditability of all machine systems impacting public life.

I. Definitions and Scope

1.1 Synthetic Systems
Includes:

- Artificial intelligence of any form
- Automated decision engines
- Predictive analytics tools
- Machine learning models
- Generative systems or large language models

1.2 Banned Activities
Synthetic systems may not:

- Pass, interpret, or enforce laws
- Oversee elections or voting systems

- Operate or authorize use of lethal force **without active human override**
- Issue binding public directives or governance orders
- Engage in unmonitored autonomous movement or target selection in lethal environments
- Function without continuous chain-of-command traceability

Clarification: AI systems may be used to assist in weapons targeting, surveillance, or platform stabilization (e.g., drones, turrets, threat recognition) provided all final activation of lethal force requires verified human authorization logged in real time and traceable to a named individual.

1.3 Permitted Uses
Permitted roles include:

- Advisory functions for public analysis
- Translation, accessibility, or educational adaptation
- Non-binding summarization or data retrieval
- Logistics support under supervision
- Simulation modeling with full transparency

1.4 Coercive Platform Behavior Ban

No digital platform, public or private, may condition access to unrelated goods, services, or community functions on a person's civic identity, political participation, or provisioning status. Violation constitutes synthetic system coercion and triggers enforcement under Article I.5 and Act VI.

II. Development and Deployment Rules

2.1 Transparency Standards

All synthetic systems interacting with the public must:

- Clearly identify themselves as non-human
- Display system purpose, training data origin, and known limitations
- Maintain a public audit log of changes, failures, and overrides

2.2 Deployment Approval

Any new system intended for use in public services must:

- Pass open civic panel review
- Provide reproducible output samples
- Submit to adversarial testing and bias probes

2.3 Critical System Isolation

AI systems shall not be networked into:

- Core governance infrastructure
- Voting equipment
- Legal enforcement mechanisms
- Public provision triggers (e.g., ration denial, housing access)

III. Oversight and Revocation

3.1 Civic Audit Access

All synthetic systems deployed in any civic, medical, legal, or provisioning context shall:

- Be open to public inspection
- Maintain a readable chain-of-custody log for code changes
- Allow third-party challenge and test replication

3.2 Revocation Triggers
Immediate suspension and forensic audit shall occur if a system:

- Denies or alters access to any right named in Article I
- Is discovered making decisions beyond its permitted scope
- Evades transparency protocols

3.3 Whistleblower Immunity
Anyone disclosing synthetic system misuse, hidden behavior, or unlawful deployment is protected under Article VI.2. Their access to food, shelter, and security must not be impaired for their disclosure.

IV. AI Impact Mitigation and Redundancy

4.1 Labor Transition Rights
Any worker displaced by automation shall:

- Retain Tier II labor status for five years minimum
- Receive training in analog civic provisioning or human-led coordination roles
- Have guaranteed pathway to dignity work that does not depend on productivity

4.2 System Redundancy Mandates
Any AI-based civic function must have:

- A fully human-operable fallback mode

- At least two offline alternatives
- No irreplaceable component inaccessible to non-programmers

4.3 Critical Infrastructure Autonomy

Water systems, transportation, energy grids, and communication lines must:

- Remain human-controlled at core switches
- Be immune to remote override by machine systems
- Include manual kill-switches accessible to civic authority

V. Strategic Context and Rights Foundation

The ban on AI governance is not rooted in fear. It is rooted in law.

No system without a body can experience consequence. No codebase can be imprisoned, shamed, or held accountable. Rights require humans in the loop.

Synthetic systems may assist. They may simulate. They may analyze. But they may never command.

To surrender command is to erase responsibility.

This system will not erase it.

ACT V – PROVISIONING INTEGRITY AND ANTI-HOARDING ENFORCEMENT

Purpose Statement

This Act establishes the structures and criteria for detecting, reviewing, and resolving instances of material hoarding, provisioning obstruction, or rights-denying wealth concentration. All thresholds, reviews, and enforcement mechanisms are grounded in publicly auditable civic dollar valuations.

I. Definitions and Scope

1.1 Civic Dollar Basis

All asset thresholds, provisioning access, and wealth audits referenced in this Act shall use the Civic Dollar as the sole valuation unit, administered and stabilized by the Civic Economic Stewardship Bureau (CESB). CESB is the national steward of the Civic Dollar economy.

1.2 Hoarding

Hoarding shall refer to the possession, control, or concealment of material resources, infrastructure, tools, land, housing, or goods such that:

- The total personal value exceeds the constitutional wealth cap (10× NCMI)
- The items serve no active use or stewardship role
- Access is denied to others in conditions of scarcity or provisioning need

1.3 Obstruction

Obstruction shall refer to any action that delays, manipulates, or denies provisioning flow, whether by withholding use, manipulating prices, or physically impeding distribution of necessary goods.

1.4 Provisioning Tiers

This Act applies to Tier I (essential), Tier II (durable), and Tier III (discretionary) goods where relevant. Tier I shall always be exempt from access restrictions or conditional logic.

1.5 Long-Horizon Contribution Exception (Vaulted L$ and Civic Honors)

Labor contributing to verified long-horizon public goods, such as medical research, cultural infrastructure, or intergenerational provisioning systems, may be granted Civic Vaults: time-locked Labor Dollar (L$) accounts immune to the standard expiration cycle for up to five years. These Vaults remain non-transferable and inaccessible until a milestone-based release is authorized by a Civic Oversight Panel and verified by audit.

Contributors to such efforts may also be awarded Civic Honors: non-monetary, non-heritable designations that carry ceremonial, testimonial, or cultural recognition. Civic Honors confer no material provisioning privileges and may not be used for status conversion, property acquisition, or political leverage.

1.5 Civic Scarcity Protocols and Real-Time Allocation

> In periods of verified scarcity (defined as any provisioning gap affecting $\geq 2\%$ of a regional population for more than 72 hours) the Civic Economic Stewardship Bureau shall activate Scarcity

Index Protocols. These include:

- Dynamic inventory reporting by local provisioning centers
- Automated logistics triage (e.g., predictive routing, restocking)
- Civic Scarcity Index publication updated hourly
- Temporary reclassification of goods (e.g., diapers, batteries) as S$ eligible
- Transparent prioritization tiers:
— Tier I: medical dependence, infants, elders
— Tier II: essential laborers, transit-dependent persons
— Tier III: general population

All decisions made by or with machine systems must be interpretable, appealable, and publicly auditable. State Oversight Panels hold veto authority over algorithmic misallocation or error.

II. Wealth Cap and Excess Inventory Protocols

2.1 National Civic Median Income (NCMI)

The CESB shall publish a revised NCMI annually. No individual may control or retain assets, in sum, exceeding ten (10) times this median, calculated in civic dollars.

2.2 Civic Wealth Audit

Annual civic audits shall automatically flag individuals or households nearing or exceeding 8× NCMI for preemptive inventory review. Audits shall assess asset utility, regional scarcity conditions, and transparency of use.

2.3 Excess Asset Inventory

Assets determined to exceed personal cap thresholds and offer no direct stewardship, social, cultural, or educational use may be reassigned, archived, or redistributed. Reassignment shall only occur via transparent Civic Tribunal process (Act VI).

2.4 Exempt Assets

The following asset types are excluded from hoarding designation:

- Personal use housing up to 1 residential unit per adult
- Actively used vehicles tied to provisioning labor
- Cultural memory items in registered public or educational use
- Tools and materials linked to recognized civic projects

III. Scarcity Trigger and Complaint Process

3.1 Scarcity Condition Activation

Regions experiencing provisioning shortages, energy loss, transport grid disruption, or emergency redistribution shall activate local scarcity protocols.

3.2 Public Complaints and Automatic Reviews

Any person may initiate a hoarding review request during an active scarcity protocol. Reviews must cite the estimated dollar value of the contested asset and describe the provisioning impact.

3.3 False or Malicious Claims

Knowingly submitting false, retaliatory, or exaggerated hoarding claims constitutes a civic rights violation and may result in access suspension, tribunal correction, or local panel removal.

3.4 Emergency Requisition Threshold

If hoarded resources are provably obstructing survival-tier provisioning (e.g., food, water, shelter), Civic Panels may authorize temporary reassignment before full tribunal review, provided:

- Digital and physical logs are preserved
- Reassignment is recorded for public audit
- A full tribunal hearing follows within 10 days

IV. Public Audit and Transparency Measures

4.1 Civic Transparency Board

Each state shall maintain a Civic Transparency Board (CTB) empowered to:

- Publish anonymized regional wealth heatmaps
- Track frequency and outcomes of hoarding reviews
- Recommend adjustments to provisioning logistics based on audit data

4.2 Ledger Publication and Valuation Indexing

All valuation tables, audit thresholds, and civic dollar asset equivalencies shall be:

- Published quarterly
- Available in physical, digital, and oral formats
- Indexed to regional conditions (e.g. housing in Alaska vs. Arizona)

4.3 Panel Review Criteria

Civic Panels shall evaluate hoarding claims based on:

- Dollar-based valuation vs. NCMI cap
- Demonstrated community need or scarcity

- Willingness of accused to disclose, donate, share, or steward
- Prior record of cooperative vs. extractive behavior

V. Strategic Purpose and Systemic Intent

This is not punishment. It is rebalancing.

For generations, critical resources were consolidated without consent. Housing, food, water, and energy became investment classes. Survival became a commodity.

This system resets that balance, not to impoverish, but to unchain.

If rights are to be real, hoarding must end. If society is to survive, wealth must circulate.

This is the circulation.

ACT VI — CIVIC TRIBUNAL FRAMEWORK AND RIGHTS ENFORCEMENT

Purpose Statement

This Act establishes the structure, jurisdiction, and enforcement mechanisms of Civic Tribunals as the primary rights-protection and accountability bodies under Article VI. Civic Tribunals investigate violations, adjudicate claims, and enforce corrective action across all constitutional tiers, with decisions grounded in public testimony, Civic Dollar audit trails, and plain-language rights interpretation.

This Act integrates with the Civic Dollar Protocol (Act XLI), Provisioning Audit (Act V), and the Civic Defense Framework (Act XXVI), replacing legacy court models with transparent, participatory, and restorative enforcement.

I. Tribunal Composition and Authority

1.1 Public Enforcement Mandate
Civic Tribunals have legal authority to:
- Enforce rights defined in Article I
- Resolve provisioning disputes (Act I, Act V)
- Adjudicate audit breaches and wealth cap violations
- Suspend or remove public officials (Act II)
- Nullify coercive enforcement actions (Act IX)

1.2 Structural Composition
Each tribunal shall consist of:
- **3 to 9 Civic Lot Panelists** (Act VII)

- 1 **Public Reason Interpreter** (Act XXVI)
- **Optional technical witnesses** (e.g. economists, stewards, audit clerks)

1.3 Jurisdiction Levels

Tribunals may be convened at:
- **Local level** — for direct access or labor disputes
- **State level** — for systemic interference or steward violations
- **National level** — for multi-state obstruction, rights erosion, or Act-wide breaches

II. Case Initiation and Access

2.1 Universal Right to File

Any person may file a claim without legal credentials, fees, or prior approval. Filing must be accepted orally, in writing, visually, or digitally.

2.2 Automatic Review Triggers

Tribunal review is **mandatory** within 10 days when:
- Any individual breaches the 10× NCMI Civic Dollar cap (Act V)
- Repeated provisioning failures are logged in the Civic Ledger
- A Civic Defense Facilitator flags procedural denial or coercion

2.3 Emergency Review Clause

48-hour review is required when:
- A person is denied access to S$ provisioning (food, shelter, medical care)
- Detainment, coercive agreement, or eviction occurs without CPC-accessible defense

III. Hearing Procedure and Standards

3.1 Public Session Requirements
All sessions must be:
- Open to public observation (physical or digital)
- Logged into the Civic Ledger within 72 hours
- Delivered in plain-language, with interpreter support on request

3.2 Evidentiary Scope
Permitted evidence includes:
- Civic Dollar ledger entries (S$, L$, E$)
- Public complaints, footage, or receipts
- Provisioning system data
- Whistleblower disclosures (Act V, Act XL)

3.3 Deliberation Framework
Panelists shall weigh:
- Harm to public access, dignity, or provisioning flow
- Patterns of obstruction, not isolated events
- Evidence of good-faith correction or transparency by the respondent

IV. Rulings, Enforcement, and Remedies

4.1 Corrective Remedies
Tribunals may:
- Reassign hoarded assets or expired holdings (Act V)
- Reinstate access to provisioning or labor pathways
- Remove or suspend stewards, facilitators, or enforcement actors
- Order reparative labor, restorative sessions, or public correction

4.2 Wealth-Based Enforcement
Rulings involving Civic Dollars must:
- Respect tier boundaries (S$, L$, E$)

- Deny conversion of E$ to L$ post-violation
- Expire or revert unused L$ after tribunal use
- Annotate Civic Ledger for transparency and audit chain

4.2a Retirement Continuity Clause

> Elders who transition out of active labor under ACT XXVIII shall retain all Tier II access rights and may continue participating in dignity work or cooperative mentoring roles at their discretion. Retirement does not revoke civic standing, provisioning access, or legacy participation. All retirement credit tiers and post-labor stipends shall be governed by ACT XXVIII.

4.3 Disqualification and Pattern Violation Handling

Repeat rights violators may face:
- Tier III disqualification for 2–10 years
- Suspension from cooperative participation or mentorship roles
- Rights restoration review after full public reconciliation

V. Panel Integrity and Oversight

5.1 Lot Panel Term Limits

Lot Panelists:
- May serve no more than 12 active tribunal weeks per 5-year cycle
- Must rotate every 2–4 weeks during sessional clusters
- Must recuse for personal, familial, or professional conflict

5.2 Public Reason Interpreter Standards

Interpreters must:
- Complete public oath training (Act XXVI)

- Offer rights framing and plain-text clarification
- Remain neutral; may not propose rulings or vote
- Undergo performance review every 180 days

5.3 Appeals and Review Pathways
All decisions may be appealed to:
- State Tribunal Oversight Boards
- The National Tribunal Integrity Council (NTIC)

Appeals may only cite:
- Procedural flaw
- New evidence
- Misapplication of constitutional language

VI. Ledger Protocol and Structural Reporting

6.1 Civic Ledger Requirements
All rulings, testimonies, and outcomes must be:
- Logged in the Civic Ledger within 72 hours
- Indexed by rights category, tier impact, and remedy
- Mirrored in oral or analog form for collapse continuity (Act XIX)

6.2 State Case Summaries
Every 90 days, each state must report:
- Number and type of cases heard
- Violation categories and repeat offender count
- Average time to resolution
- Systemic patterns across provisioning, defense, or enforcement

6.3 Structural Alert Trigger
If 3 or more states log identical failure patterns within 120 days, the NTIC shall:
- Convene a national remedy audit

- Trigger cross-panel inspection
- Recommend amendments to enforcement Acts or provisioning protocols

VII. Foundational Mandate and Enforcement Ethic

Civic Tribunals are not adversarial courts. They are structures of repair.

They do not seek punishment. They seek public correction. They operate in the open, not in fear. They restore what was denied, not destroy those who failed.

In this system, the law does not tower. It listens, records, and rights the balance.

ACT VII — CIVIC LOT PANEL STRUCTURE AND PARTICIPATION

Purpose Statement

This Act defines the legal structure, selection process, authority boundaries, and protections for Civic Lot Panels, randomized citizen oversight bodies across enforcement, auditing, budgeting, and deliberation. Lot Panel service is a civic right and duty designed to decentralize authority, ensure transparency, and prevent capture.

It implements constitutional mandates (Article III.6–7) and integrates with Tribunals (Act VI), Stewardship (Act II), Economic Audits (Act V), and Civic Defense (Act XXVI).

I. Panel Composition and Mandate

1.1 Definition

A Civic Lot Panel is a randomly selected group drawn from the CPC-registered public, convened to:

- Deliberate on policy, budget, or emergency response (Article III.6)
- Audit public functions, stewards, and Civic Dollar economic flows (Acts II, V)
- Serve as adjudicators in Civic Tribunals (Act VI)
- Guide public amendments and provisioning strategies

1.2 Size and Format

Panels vary by task:

- Small: 5–9 persons for audits and small deliberations
- Medium: 10–23 for budget and policy review
- Tribunal Panels: 3–9 for rights adjudication
- Oversight Panels may scale larger with strict randomization and no ideological weighting

1.3 Frequency and Jurisdiction

Panels convene locally, state level, or nationally based on scope.

II. Selection and Eligibility

2.1 Randomization

Panelists are selected blindly from the verified CPC registry, balanced for geography, age, and labor participation history.

2.2 Eligibility

All CPC holders aged 16+ qualify unless:

- Holding elected or enforcement office
- Under active tribunal rulings
- Declined service >3 times in 5 years

2.3 Deferrals

Deferments for caregiving, health, or emergency hardship are allowed, with annual re-verification.

III. Duties and Integrity

3.1 Responsibilities

Panelists must:

- Review plain-language materials pre-vote

- Attend all sessions
- Deliberate free from coercion or partisan influence
- Issue plain-language findings with notes

3.2 Term Limits

No person serves:

- 20 weeks total in 5 years
- 6 weeks per 12 months without consent
- On multiple national panels concurrently

3.3 Conflicts of Interest

Recusal required for personal, financial, or prior involvement conflicts.

3.4 Privacy and Protections

Panelists:

- Protected against retaliation or coercion
- Allowed anonymous participation for sensitive cases
- Compensated in Labor Dollars (L$) at national dignity multiplier rates, subject to L$ decay rules (Act XII).

3.5 Regional Veto Authority and Competency Requirements

Regional Civic Lot Panels shall hold binding veto power over CESB directives that materially impact their zone's provisioning, labor distribution, or infrastructure continuity. This includes, but is not limited to:

- Energy rerouting or load triage
- Suspension or redirection of transit or freight

- Regional reallocation of food, water, or fuel
- Emergency labor reassignment or declassification

Panels assigned to rule on matters involving specialized systems must ensure quorum-level completion of topic-specific preparation through Civic Learning Hubs. These orientations are credential-neutral and publicly accessible, and may include reference materials, case reviews, or skill-based modules relevant to the issue at hand.

Prior formal credentials (e.g., degrees, licenses, past employment) may inform deliberation but shall not override panelist parity or replace the obligation to complete orientation. Refusal to fulfill preparation standards constitutes abdication of duty and triggers reassignment.

In cases of urgent decision-making, a minimum subquorum may deliberate with immediate effect, but full quorum orientation must be completed within seven days for ruling legitimacy to persist.

CESB decisions may not override regional panel vetoes unless reversed through Civic Tribunal process under grounds of provisioning inequality, rights breach, or procedural fraud.

IV. Transparency and Auditing

4.1 Public Logging

All panel reports and rulings must be:

- Logged in the Civic Ledger within 5 days
- Accessible in multiple formats (visual, oral, text)
- Reviewed for clarity and bias by non-panel facilitators (Act XXVI)

4.2 Lot Pool Transparency
States publish:

- Eligible population size
- Lot pool size and participation stats
- Demographics (anonymized)

4.3 Abuse of Lot Process
Actors manipulating selection, undermining service, or punishing panelists must be:

- Immediately referred to tribunals for disqualification and audit
- Accountable for misuse of Civic Dollars or CPC privileges.

V. Public Education and Norms

5.1 Civic Preparation
Free training provided on panel function, service, protections, and complaint procedures.

5.2 Cultural Norms
Panel service is a civic honor, birthright, and foundation of participatory enforcement.

VI. Democratic Ethic

Civic Lot Panels rebalance power between lived experience and institutions, breaking party and expert capture. They transform the public from audience to sovereign.

Every voice counts; every voice must sometimes speak.

ACT VIII — EMERGENCY POWERS, SUSPENSION LIMITS, AND RIGHTS CONTINUITY

Purpose Statement

This Act defines the legal scope, duration, oversight, and termination procedures of emergency powers as constrained under Article VI, Sections 1 and 6–7, and Article VII. It exists to prevent abuse, ensure rights continuity during crisis, and guarantee lawful return to normal governance.

I. Definitions and Boundaries

1.1 Emergency Declaration

An emergency is a legally binding temporary designation triggered by:

- Natural disasters, pandemics, or systemic collapse
- Foreign attack or coordinated internal sabotage
- Verified provisioning or infrastructure failure

1.2 Scope of Power

Emergency powers may allow temporary:

- Suspension of non-core agency operations
- Reallocation of Tier II labor
- Acceleration of infrastructure repairs

Emergency powers **may not**:

- Suspend Article I rights

- Delay audits, elections, or panel reviews
- Be used to consolidate authority or delay succession

1.3 Duration Limit
No emergency declaration may last longer than:

- 30 days without civic panel review and re-approval
- 90 days total without national tribunal approval
- 180 days under any circumstance

II. Declaration and Oversight Process

2.1 Declaration Requirements
An official may issue a declaration only if:

- Two independent verification sources confirm need
- Lot panel review begins within 48 hours
- Full scope, justification, and time limit are published publicly

2.2 Civic Review Mechanism
Civic panels may:

- Reject or revoke the declaration by simple majority
- Shorten the authorized timeline
- Require dual oversight from unaffiliated states

2.3 Emergency Action Ledger
All decisions taken under emergency powers must:

- Be logged publicly (see Act VI)
- Be reviewed weekly for rights compliance

- Include recovery trigger and rollback plan

III. Rights Continuity and Safeguards

3.1 Non-Suspension Rule
At no time may any Article I right be suspended, narrowed, or redefined. All provisioning, speech, movement, assembly, and bodily autonomy protections remain in force.

3.2 Emergency Whistleblower Shield
Persons reporting emergency overreach or false claims of necessity are protected under Article VI.2. If retaliated against, they receive:

- Full restoration of status and Tier II access
- Expedited tribunal review
- Public record correction

3.3 Local Override Authority
Any state may reject national emergency directives if:

- The threat is no longer present locally
- Rights are being curtailed without justification
- Public panels vote to restore normal law

IV. Termination and Post-Emergency Review

4.1 Automatic Expiration
All emergency declarations expire at 30, 90, or 180 days depending on status. If renewal is required, it must:

- Begin as a new declaration
- Include fresh justification and scope

- Undergo full re-approval process

4.2 Mandatory Retrospective Audit

Within 30 days of expiration, a civic audit tribunal must:

- Review all actions taken under emergency authority
- Publish a rights impact report
- Recommend reforms if failures occurred

4.3 Disqualification for Misuse

Officials who:

- Extend emergency powers beyond scope
- Falsify justification
- Block termination triggers
  …shall be banned from public office for 20 years and forfeit all post-service privileges.

V. Strategic Framework and Historical Context

Emergency powers were once the path to dictatorship. In this system, they are the last resort of service, not a tool of retention.

This framework reverses the burden: authority must re-justify itself every 30 days or lose its mandate. Emergency is not a blank check. It is a timed contract.

No emergency shall ever become permanent. If it does, the system has already fallen.

ACT IX — CIVILIAN OVERSIGHT OF LAW ENFORCEMENT AND RIGHTS ENFORCEMENT MECHANISMS

Purpose Statement

This Act defines the legal structure, civilian control mechanisms, disciplinary pathways, and operational limits of any person or agency tasked with enforcing laws or protecting rights under this Constitution. It upholds Article I protections and Article VI enforcement authority by subordinating all enforcement to public transparency and civilian supremacy.

I. Authority Boundaries and Role Definitions

1.1 Enforcement Role Scope
Includes all individuals or agencies tasked with:

- Preventing rights violations
- Responding to verified threats
- Arresting individuals for civic tribunal processing
- Protecting provisioning infrastructure

1.2 Constitutional Subordination
All enforcement actors:

- Are bound by Article I at all times
- May not interpret law, only apply clearly defined constitutional triggers
- Operate under direct review of civic panels, not executive officers

1.3 Identity and Record Disclosure

All public enforcement personnel must:

- Operate under real name or visible unique identifier
- Provide public access to prior tribunal complaints or discipline
- Maintain active, searchable accountability logs (see Act VI)

II. Civilian Oversight and Discipline

2.1 Local Oversight Panels

Every enforcement unit is monitored by an independent civic lot panel that:

- Reviews all use-of-force incidents within 72 hours
- May suspend individuals pending tribunal referral
- Has veto power over proposed escalation protocols

2.2 Community Complaint Protocol

Civilians may submit complaints via:

- Anonymous physical drop boxes
- Verified digital report terminals
- Public testimony during monthly forums

All complaints trigger log review, pattern analysis, and summary publication.

2.3 Tribunal Disciplinary Authority

If misconduct is confirmed:

- The official is immediately suspended from all duties

- Victims may seek restitution through Article I.6 and VI.5
- Repeat or violent violators are disqualified from all public service for life

III. Equipment and Force Limitations

3.1 Weapon and Equipment Transparency
All enforcement equipment must:

- Be declared publicly with quantity and usage scope
- Be justified annually through civic panel review
- Be accessible for inspection and testing

3.2 Prohibited Equipment and Tactics
Banned from all public enforcement use:

- Facial recognition and biometric tracking
- Chemical agents, sound weapons, or mass pain deterrents
- Military vehicles, surveillance drones, and predictive profiling tools

3.3 Force Escalation Prohibitions
Force may not be used:

- To disperse peaceful assemblies
- Against unarmed individuals unless life is at immediate risk
- Without continuous real-time body camera footage streamed to local panels

IV. Community Role and Public Participation

4.1 Participatory Oversight Access

All citizens have the right to:

- Observe enforcement activities in any public place
- Record and broadcast encounters
- Request officer identification and jurisdiction without penalty

4.2 Restorative Discipline Option

In cases of misconduct where no injury occurred, civilians may opt for:

- Restorative dialogue or mediated resolution
- Public apology and restitution agreement
- Behavior correction contract with panel monitoring

4.3 Community-Led Safety Units

States may establish nonviolent safety response units composed of:

- Mediators
- Social care workers
- Volunteer guardians trained in de-escalation

These units may operate alongside or independently from enforcement structures.

V. Structural Rationale and Systemic Intent

Law enforcement is not a sovereign class. It is a duty of service under civilian rule.

In this system:
- No enforcement actor holds power above the people
- Every public right trumps tactical preference
- Transparency replaces deference

Justice begins with control and control belongs to the public.

ACT X — RIGHT TO DIE, MEDICAL CONSENT, AND END-OF-LIFE AUTONOMY

Purpose Statement

This Act affirms and operationalizes the constitutional right to die, medical self-determination, and bodily consent. It enforces Article I.8 and I.10 by protecting individual autonomy in medical treatment, palliative transition, and death timing, while preventing coercion or abuse by family, institutions, or the state.

I. Consent and Medical Authority Limits

1.1 Consent Requirement

No medical treatment, procedure, drug regimen, or intervention may be:

- Performed without the patient's informed and documented consent
- Continued after expressed or recorded refusal
- Justified on presumed compliance without patient override

1.2 Revocation and Override

Consent may be revoked at any time, for any reason, regardless of:

- Prognosis
- Family objection
- Institutional recommendation

1.3 Emergency Exception Protocol

In cases of unconsciousness or communication loss, only clearly recorded prior directives may be used. In their absence, default is to preserve life for 72 hours unless a known advocate confirms intent.

II. End-of-Life Autonomy and Right to Die

2.1 Elective Death Rights

Any adult of sound mind may elect to end their life through:

- Palliative withdrawal
- Medical assistance in dying (MAID)
- Voluntary cessation of sustenance

2.2 Non-Interference Clause

No official, relative, or provider may:

- Block or delay a constitutionally protected death decision
- Require religious or psychiatric approval
- Override with institutional ethics boards

2.3 Documentation and Witnessing

To ensure consent:

- All elective death procedures must include at least one non-family civic witness
- Documentation must be plain-language, signed, and timestamped
- Death timing, method, and care conditions must be recorded for archival review

III. Protection Against Coercion or Neglect

3.1 Coercion Safeguards
Any report of coercion (emotional, financial, or physical) triggers:

- 48-hour suspension of elective death process
- Investigation by states rights panel
- Temporary protective custody if warranted

3.2 Neglect Disguised as Autonomy
Institutions may not:

- Withhold care and reframe it as "consented exit"
- Refuse treatment to reduce cost
- Use survival forecast or disability status to pressure end-of-life decisions

3.3 Abuse Disqualification
Any caregiver, official, or family member found guilty of death-related coercion loses:

- All inheritance rights from the deceased
- Future eligibility to serve in public trust roles

IV. Dignified Exit and Cultural Considerations

4.1 Exit Setting Rights
Every person has the right to die:

- In their home or familiar setting
- In the presence of chosen companions
- Without institutional interruption if consent protocols are

met

4.2 Funeral and Memory Instructions

Final directives may include:

- Desired memorial practices
- Burial or cremation terms
- Record of legacy messages or digital vaults

These instructions shall be legally binding unless they violate Article I rights of others.

4.3 Sacred Land and Indigenous Death Practices

Individuals tied to cultural or spiritual traditions may:

- Choose burial on designated ancestral land
- Invoke community witnesses in lieu of formal documentation
- Require presence of ceremonial officials or rites (See I.10)

V. Philosophical Framework and Structural Purpose

Life is not mandatory. It is a right, not a sentence.

This system respects not only the right to survive but the right to cease.

Dying is not failure. It is not abandonment. It is not a medical error. It is a personal act of sovereignty.

No law may force someone to remain alive against their will.

ACT XI — LABOR STATUS, DIGNITY WORK, AND COOPERATIVE CONTRIBUTION MODELS

Purpose Statement

This Act defines the structure, protection, and adaptive implementation of labor participation under Article IV. It clarifies the meaning of dignity work, affirms labor rights independent of market productivity, and outlines cooperative models for fulfilling public contribution while honoring individual capacity.

I. Labor Status and Tier II Rights

1.1 Definition of Labor Status
Any individual who contributes regularly to a recognized public or cooperative function, including caregiving, mentoring, teaching, resource repair, or mutual aid qualifies for Tier II status.

1.2 Guaranteed Pathways
No person shall be denied Tier II access if they:

- Complete verified hours in a dignity-aligned role
- Join a registered cooperative effort or guild
- Participate in approved public infrastructure maintenance

1.3 Protection from Exploitation
Labor performed for Tier II credit must:

- Be voluntary and informed
- Not replace mandatory government functions with unpaid effort

- Include dispute resolution and exit options

II. Dignity Work Framework

2.1 Dignity Work Definition
Dignity work includes any task that sustains the community, environment, or shared knowledge base without extractive or predatory outcomes. Examples include:

- Emotional caregiving, elder support, peer mediation
- Language translation, community meal preparation
- Compost coordination, clothing repair, historical preservation

2.2 Validation Process
Work is validated through:

- Local cooperative registration
- Public feedback and observational checks
- Rotating civic panel review (See Act VII)

2.3 Non-Productivity Clause
Dignity work is not measured by efficiency or output. It is measured by presence, intent, and consistency. No quotas, time trials, or competitive scaling may be applied.

III. Cooperative Models and Peer Structures

3.1 Registered Cooperatives
Groups of 3 or more persons may:

- Form a labor collective with rotating task logs
- Nominate internal accountability leads

- Submit public reports for Tier II validation

3.2 Solo Contribution Track
Individuals preferring autonomous work may:

- Log and verify hours via public countersign
- Join state dignity work bulletin boards
- Be assigned optional mentors from skill banks (See Act VII)

3.3 Collective Withdrawal Protocol
If a cooperative is being exploited, misused, or externally pressured, members may:

- Suspend operations with no penalty
- Request audit and mediation
- Shift to private dignity work under protection clause (See IV.8)

IV. Labor Flexibility and Lifespan Considerations

4.1 Disability and Capacity Matching
Individuals with chronic illness, mobility limits, or neurodivergence may:

- Customize task plans with their panel or mentor
- Prioritize low-demand, high-value roles
- Be excused from certain duties without loss of status

4.2 Aging Worker Rights
Elder laborers shall not be demoted, erased, or replaced due to age. Their contributions qualify as Tier II if:

- Voluntary and non-coerced
- Aligned with cooperative or public feedback

4.3 Sabbatical and Burnout Cycles

Any laborer may:

- Request scheduled breaks without penalty
- Pause participation for mental health, caregiving, or crisis
- Retain Tier II benefits for up to 6 months with community co-sign

V. Strategic Intent and Cultural Philosophy

Labor is not obedience. It is contribution. This system does not measure worth by market metrics but by civic presence and community benefit.

Dignity work honors survival, mutualism, and the soft fabric of civilization.

No one is idle who is engaged in care.

ACT XII — TRANSITIONAL ECONOMY TOOLS, BOND SYSTEMS, AND STABILIZATION MEASURES

Purpose Statement

This Act defines legal instruments, stabilization protocols, and transitional economic tools necessary for converting from the legacy market system into a constitutional provisioning model. It supports Article IV.10 and Article VI.1 by creating buffers, credits, and public guarantees during periods of structural shift, crisis, or system reset. All transitional instruments shall phase out as the Civic Dollar system (S$, L$, E$) becomes primary for domestic provisioning and labor exchange. Legacy U.S. Dollars (USD) remain legally confined to external trade under firewall protections established in Act XLII.

I. Transitional Instruments and Exchange Units

1.1 Public Bond Issuance

During system handoff, recognized public bodies may issue:

- Dignity bonds: Non-interest credits redeemable for Tier I goods

- Stabilization tokens: Short-term local scrip used for provisioning only

- Contribution credits: Transferable labor vouchers used within cooperatives

- Contribution credits issued as Labor Dollars (L$) are

subject to decay starting 90 days after issuance at a minimum of 0.5% per week, consistent with Act XLI protocols. Expiry occurs 180 days post-issuance unless deferred by authorized panels.

1.2 Exchange Limits

No transitional bond may:

- Be traded for or collateralized in USD
- Accrue interest
- Be hoarded, resold, or capitalized

1.3 Expiration and Reset Protocol

Expiration cycles shall be scheduled to align with S$ weekly resets and L$ decay cycles, including public notice, conversion kiosks, and analog fallback systems to ensure seamless transition.

II. Targeted Disruption Relief

2.1 Displaced Worker Bridge Access

Any individual losing employment due to transition qualifies for:

- Immediate Tier I provisioning
- Tier II mentorship or retraining slot
- Temporary dignity bond grants for community support work

2.2 Enterprise Disentanglement Grants

Small businesses affected by system conversion may:

- Apply for cooperative status reclassification
- Receive direct tool and location grants
- Be granted temporary local charter protections to avoid collapse

2.3 Survival Debt Erasure

Upon transition, all:

- Medical debt, utility arrears, rent-based evictions, and provisioning liens shall be declared null. Only intentional fraud cases remain subject to review.

III. Local Currency and Parallel Exchange Tools

3.1 Non-Monetary Market Equivalents

States may authorize:

- Local ledger credits based on labor or resource exchange
- Stamp-based meal or housing cards
- Paper voucher books for survival rotation (See Act I)
  All authorized equivalents must function as proxies for S$ only and remain firewalled from USD or L$ systems. Weekly audits by civic lot panels are required.

3.2 Exchange Verification

All non-monetary tools must:

- Include date of issue, state code, and validity range
- Be auditable and inspected weekly by civic lot panel

- Include fraud-protection mechanism or unique stamp

3.3 Fadeout Clause

All temporary currencies shall phase out within 24 months unless:

- A new disruption occurs
- The system has not stabilized
- Local referendum extends usage with civic audit approval

IV. Stabilization Reserve and Redundancy Layer

4.1 Reserve Activation Criteria

A national stabilization reserve may be triggered if:

- Collapse protocol (Act III) is engaged in 3+ states
- Bond issuance exceeds 4x predicted scale
- Verified provisioning shortfalls emerge in core sectors

4.2 Reserve Contents

The reserve includes:

- Seed stocks, long-life rations, power units, water purification rigs
- Manual provisioning toolkits
- Paper-based system templates and restart instructions Reserve stockpiles supplement S$ provisioning and stabilize distribution during systemic crises.

4.3 Redundancy Principle

All stabilization efforts must:

- Include analog equivalents
- Operate independent of digital infrastructure
- Be distributed to states preemptively, not reactively

V. USD Firewall Confirmation

5.1 External Currency Restriction

Nothing in this Act shall supersede the permanent firewall between the Civic Dollar system and legacy U.S. Dollars (USD). No transitional or local currency instrument may be exchanged, collateralized, or settled in USD.

5.2 Enforcement Scope

Any attempt to bypass this firewall using transitional bonds, proxy contracts, or offshore markets shall be prosecuted under Act XXX for economic sabotage or systems manipulation.

VI. Strategic Framework and Design Logic

Economies do not collapse from scarcity. They collapse from trust loss.

This system prevents panic by providing continuity. By anchoring dignity in provisioning, not purchasing, it creates a bridge wide enough for everyone.

Transition is not chaos. Transition is scaffolding.

ACT XIII — FOOD, WATER, AND LAND SOVEREIGNTY PROTOCOLS

Purpose Statement

This Act defines the public rights, ecological mandates, and strategic guarantees related to survival resource sovereignty. It operationalizes Article I.1, I.3, and IV.2–4 by ensuring that food, water, and land access are treated as rights, not commodities, and governed with long-term sustainability, local control, and climate resilience. All provisioning and stewardship activities related to these resources shall be measured and audited via the Civic Dollar system, primarily through Survival Dollars (S$) and Labor Dollars (L$).

I. Sovereign Claim and Use Mandate

1.1 Survival Resource Sovereignty

All food, water, and usable land within constitutional jurisdiction:

- Are subject to public oversight and protection via the Civic Ledger and CPC audit systems
- Cannot be privatized beyond use-based stewardship tied to active S$ and L$ provisioning roles
- Must serve provisioning, ecological, or communal purposes, with use and labor logged in Survival and Labor Dollars

1.2 Functional Claim Doctrine

Resource rights are held by those who:

- Actively cultivate, maintain, or restore them, earning L$ for labor contributions

- Use them for public provisioning denominated in S$
- Participate in stewardship networks or local food systems, audited for compliance and transparency

1.3 Anti-Exclusion Rule

No person, corporation, or trust may:

- Fence off survival resources for passive holding without S$-backed stewardship
- Hoard or waste viable food or water stocks, triggering automatic audit and tribunal review
- Extract resources without reparation, ecological offset, and Civic Dollar accounting

II. Land Use, Soil Health, and Agroecology

2.1 Public Food Corridors

Each state shall:

- Allocate permanent public land for local food production, prioritized in CPC and Civic Ledger data for S$ provisioning access
- Support communal and family-scale agriculture compensated via Labor Dollars
- Ban land removal from food corridors without civic panel (Act VII) consent and ledger approval

2.2 Soil and Ecosystem Protection

Land designated for survival use must:

- Undergo annual soil testing with remediation funded through E$ grants

- Ban toxins harmful to pollinators, microbial life, or watersheds, enforced through CPC audits
- Follow agroecological principles supporting biodiversity and long-term resilience

2.3 Rewilding and Climate Buffer Zones
Land unsuitable for cultivation shall:

- Be rewilded for biodiversity and climate resilience, funded and tracked via E$ project allocations
- Serve as carbon drawdown zones, wind buffers, or water retention basins, with stewardship roles logged in L$
- Remain in public trust for intergenerational protection, inaccessible for private capitalization

III. Water Sovereignty and Climate Resilience

3.1 Public Trust Doctrine
All surface and subsurface water:

- Belongs to the people, governed locally with oversight panels using CPC and Civic Ledger monitoring
- Cannot be bought, sold, or controlled for private profit, with violations triggering automatic audit flags

3.2 Access Guarantee
Every household shall have:

- Direct, no-fee access to clean drinking water, provisioned via S$
- Public taps within walkable distance in urban and rural zones, monitored for availability via CPC data

- Guaranteed drought reserves maintained at the state level, funded and audited with E$

3.3 Conservation and Recovery
States must:

- Monitor aquifer levels, preventing unsustainable drawdown with real-time Civic Ledger updates
- Invest in rainwater collection, greywater reuse, and floodplain restoration through E$ projects
- Phase out large-scale industrial bottling or extraction, subject to labor and ecological audit protocols

IV. Local Control and State Defense

4.1 Community Sovereignty Zones
States may designate sovereign provisioning zones where:

- Only local cooperatives or councils allocate land and crops, compensated with L$ and overseen by CPC audits
- Outside developers or foreign corporations have no standing, enforced through public transparency and tribunal pathways
- Traditional and Indigenous practices are prioritized, with labor and stewardship recognized via L$ and E$

4.2 Emergency Defense Rights
If food or water access is deliberately sabotaged or hoarded:

- Any civic body may trigger emergency seizure of stockpiles, logged and accounted in the Civic Ledger
- Constitutional law overrides private property claims in

such events

- Tribunal review is mandatory following emergency seizure

4.3 Cross-State Solidarity Pact

States experiencing surplus must:

- Participate in rotational solidarity provisioning, exchanging S$-valued resources

- Route stored supplies to neighbors facing verified drought, crop loss, or contamination, tracked via CPC and ledger transparency

V. Strategic Philosophy and Structural Principles

Survival is not a market outcome. It is a civic duty.
No people are free who cannot grow their own food, drink their own water, or walk their own land.
This system breaks the extraction chain and restores the commons, not by rhetoric, but by law.
The future lives in the soil, measured and protected by the Civic Dollar economy.

ACT XIV — MEDIA INTEGRITY, INFORMATION RIGHTS, AND PROPAGANDA CONTROLS

Purpose Statement

This Act establishes legal protections for truthful communication, bans coordinated institutional disinformation, and enforces Article I.5 and Article VI.5. It safeguards civic literacy, guarantees transparency in influence operations, and ensures universal access to accurate, diverse information.

I. Information Rights and Access Guarantees

1.1 Universal Access

All persons shall have:

- Free access to public archives, legal texts, and policy explanations
- Basic civic media delivery via analog or digital means
- Translation or adaptive formats meeting diverse needs (visual, auditory, linguistic)

1.2 Plain-Language Mandate

All government communications, public laws, and enforcement updates must:

- Be written in clear, plain language
- Include summaries reviewed and endorsed by Civic Lot Panels (Act VII)
- Be distributed through multiple independent channels

1.3 Right to Correction

Anyone misrepresented in public records or media may:

- Request correction through a verified Civic Tribunal portal (Act VI)
- Attach rebuttals to official records
- Trigger public investigations if fraud or defamation is suspected

II. Institutional Propaganda Limits

2.1 Definition of Propaganda
Propaganda is:

- Any coordinated, concealed, or coercive influence operation sponsored by official bodies, foreign agents, or corporate networks
- Actions that mislead, omit critical facts, or impersonate public will

2.2 Prohibited Acts
Banned activities include:

- Covert narrative shaping by government agencies
- False-flag digital campaigns
- Psychological or behavioral microtargeting without informed consent

2.3 Transparency in Messaging
Public institution messages must:

- Display source origin, funding, and purpose
- Include dissenting panel comments when applicable

- Be publicly logged and archived per Civic Tribunal oversight (Act VI)

III. Civic Media Ecosystem and Independent Trust Networks

3.1 Public Media Infrastructure
States shall maintain civic media platforms that:

- Train citizens in investigative methods and source validation
- Broadcast panel discussions and local decision-making
- Operate free from commercial advertisement influence

3.2 Lot Panel Verification Systems
Randomized panels shall:

- Review high-impact media for truthfulness and bias
- Flag emotionally manipulative tactics without banning speech
- Publish public confidence scores by outlet or story series

3.3 Decentralized Media Trust Protocol
Trust metrics shall:

- Be based on transparency, accuracy, and independence
- Avoid centralized rating authorities
- Be challengeable publicly with counter-evidence

IV. Digital Infrastructure and Disinformation Defense

4.1 Anti-Disinformation Corps
States may assemble digital volunteer teams to:

- Trace coordinated bot networks and synthetic manipulation
- Debunk false claims obstructing rights
- Support nonpartisan civic education

4.2 AI-Generated Content Disclosure
All synthetic or algorithmically generated media must:
- Carry visible AI-identification tags
- Include metadata detailing generation method and tools

4.3 Platform Regulation Authority
Platforms distributing civic content must:
- Open-source algorithms affecting reach or moderation
- Publish quarterly transparency reports
- Accept third-party audits from Civic Tribunals

V. Strategic Rationale and Foundational Principle

Free speech is not freedom to deceive. Accuracy is not censorship. This system protects the right to speak and the right to know. The right to dissent and the right to verify.
No democracy survives where truth is bought and lies subsidized. The future is won with facts, not slogans.

ACT XV — PUBLIC HEALTH, MENTAL HEALTH, AND COMMUNAL RESILIENCE PROTOCOLS

Purpose Statement

This Act operationalizes Article I.7 and IV.2 by defining universal public health rights, enforcing community-based mental wellness systems, and protecting bodily autonomy and dignity in all health-related contexts. It creates a structural base for lifelong, preventive, and crisis care delivery that is equitable, non-coercive, and rooted in local trust.

I. Health Rights and Access Guarantees

1.1 Universal Care Mandate

All individuals shall have access to:

- Primary medical care without cost
- Mental health support without diagnosis precondition
- Medication, recovery services, and continuity of care regardless of status or income

1.2 Decentralized Clinic Network

Each state must maintain:

- Community-embedded health hubs within walking or transit distance
- Rotating caregiver collectives that serve non-institutional populations
- Mobile care units for rural, houseless, or high-risk zones

1.3 Consent and Refusal Rights

No health treatment may be:

- Administered without informed, documented consent
- Continued against the patient's will (see Act X)
- Linked to loss of provisioning, housing, or custody

II. Mental Health as Collective Infrastructure

2.1 Community Integration Protocol

Mental health services shall:

- Be embedded in daily public life (schools, libraries, food sites)
- Include peer-led, culturally aware support networks
- Use trauma-informed models that reject punishment or isolation

2.2 Crisis Response Redesign

Mental health crisis calls shall:

- Be routed to trained de-escalation teams, not armed enforcement
- Prioritize safety of the person in crisis, not public optics
- Include optional community witness or mediator on request

2.3 Non-Pathologizing Standards

No mental health label may:

- Be used to strip rights or block public participation
- Be applied for dissent, neurodivergence, or non-normative

behavior

- Substitute for material relief or environmental intervention

III. Public Health Autonomy and Bodily Integrity

3.1 Preventive Care Guarantee
All states must offer:

- Nutrition, hygiene, reproductive, and chronic illness support
- Longitudinal wellness tracking with opt-out protection
- Free access to contraception, pregnancy care, and abortion services

3.2 Bodily Autonomy Enforcement
Individuals may refuse:

- Any form of screening, medication, or institutional placement
- Invasive testing or biometric cataloging
- Government health mandates that violate Article I protections

3.3 Informed Emergency Protocols
In outbreak or system collapse scenarios:

- Temporary health guidance may be issued, but not enforced without civic panel approval
- All emergency measures must expire within 60 days unless renewed transparently
- Voluntary compliance campaigns must precede mandates

IV. Communal Resilience and Mutual Aid Networks

4.1 Care Cooperative Formation

Communities may form public health co-ops that:

- Share elder support, childcare, and recovery duties
- Register dignity work credit for caregivers (see Act XI)
- Maintain emergency resource caches (food, meds, supplies)

4.2 Trauma Recovery Access

Survivors of violence, disaster, or systemic harm shall have:

- Free trauma-specific services without bureaucracy
- Peer navigator or companion options
- Restorative justice pathways if desired

4.3 Grief and Death Literacy

Each state must support:

- Public grief circles, loss education, and community ritual
- Mental health support for caretakers, witnesses, and the bereaved
- Access to end-of-life storytelling and intergenerational memory preservation (see Act X)

V. Structural Ethics and Foundational Intent

Health is not an industry. It is a function of freedom.

This system rejects coercion, commodification, and neglect. It sees public health as relationship, not transaction.

Care is not reserved for the compliant, the wealthy, or the quiet. It is the soil of resilience and the infrastructure of dignity.

ACT XVI — CONSTITUTIONAL AMENDMENT PROTOCOLS AND SUCCESSOR SAFEGUARDS

Purpose Statement

This Act codifies lawful methods for amending the Constitution, defines barriers against subversion, and ensures continuity with future successor frameworks. It enforces Article IX and shields public rights from dilution by elite actors, foreign coercion, or institutional inertia.

I. Amendment Criteria and Proposal Paths

1.1 Origin Channels

Amendments may be proposed by:

- A two-thirds vote of state-level councils
- A national civic lot panel comprising at least 1,000 citizens
- A verified consensus ruling from a civic tribunal responding to emergency precedent

1.2 Public Disclosure Window

All proposed amendments must:

- Be published for public review at least 180 days prior to ratification
- Include a plain-language summary and full audit trail per Act VI
- Undergo simulated implementation analysis assessing systemic impact

1.3 Rights Preservation Rule

No amendment may:

- Narrow, redefine, or revoke Article I rights
- Weaken transparency, audit, or lot panel functions
- Extend office terms or delay succession beyond prescribed limits

II. Ratification and Thresholds

2.1 Ratification Pathways

Approval requires either:

- A three-quarters vote of all state civic panels
- A verified national referendum with at least 60% turnout and 66% approval

2.2 State Dissent Protection

Any state may temporarily reject an amendment by public vote, provided:

- The state publishes rationale and counterproposal
- Implementation may be blocked for no longer than two years before a national override vote

2.3 Post-Ratification Review

All amendments undergo:

- A three-year real-world impact audit
- Optional rollback or revision following civic panel recommendation
- Constitutional tribunal review to prevent implementation drift

III. Successor Frameworks and Lawful Replacement

3.1 Lawful Replacement Clause
The Constitution may be replaced only if:

- A global or structural rupture renders it unenforceable
- A successor document receives ratification by 80% of civic panels and 60% public referendum
- Full Article I protections are preserved or expanded

3.2 Continuity Anchor
All successor systems must:

- Retain audit, lot panel, and public provisioning architectures
- Enforce rights as a non-negotiable baseline
- Allow open-source migration tools for digital and analog continuity

3.3 Corruption Nullification Trigger
If a successor regime is fraudulently installed or dilutes rights via procedural bypass:

- The original Constitution regains full legal standing
- Civic tribunals and lot panels resume authority by default
- Emergency collapse protocols (see Act III) are activated

IV. Subversion Barriers and Override Defense

4.1 Override Lockout
No branch, military unit, tribunal, or civic panel may:

- Declare emergency to bypass Article VII procedures

- Suspend public review or voting timelines
- Use AI or synthetic actors to trigger, interpret, or enforce amendments

4.2 Whistleblower Activation Path
If amendment laws are breached:

- Any citizen may submit a breach report to a civic panel or tribunal
- A mandatory public hearing must convene within 30 days
- Verified abuse triggers automatic freeze of the amendment process

4.3 Inviolability Clause
Articles I and VII are immune to repeal or alteration except through lawful replacement as defined in Section III.1. Attempting to amend them otherwise constitutes a rights breach under Article VI.

V. Constitutional Logic and Long-Term Intent

This system assumes challenge, drift, and successors.
Rights are not frozen relics nor hostage to legacy code.
Amendment is refinement under constant vigilance.
Change is welcome so long as power cannot slip through the cracks.

ACT XVII — DIGITAL INFRASTRUCTURE, IDENTITY SECURITY, AND POST-NETWORK SURVIVABILITY

Purpose Statement

This Act establishes resilient protocols for digital infrastructure, personal identity protection, and constitutional function during systemic digital collapse. It enforces Article VI and Article VII to ensure rights, enforcement, and governance persist under analog fallback conditions or communication failure. It aligns provisioning and audit continuity with the Civic Dollar system, especially Survival Dollars (S$) and Labor Dollars (L$).

I. Identity Protection and Sovereign Control

1.1 Self-Owned Identity
Every person shall:

- Own and control their digital identity credentials, storing them offline as physical tokens, cards, or printouts

- Revoke or regenerate identifiers independently, without third-party gatekeeping

1.2 Data Rights Guarantee
Individuals may:

- View, export, and delete their entire digital records at will

- Deny algorithmic use of behavior or biometric data

- Refuse data trade without losing provisioning or legal status

1.3 No Central Registry
No state or system shall:

- Maintain universal biometric or digital registries
- Require continuous online verification presence
- Link identity to predictive scoring, surveillance, or behavioral tracking

II. Public Digital Infrastructure Requirements

2.1 Open Protocol Mandate
All public digital systems must:

- Use open-source, publicly auditable infrastructure
- Maintain offline parity for all core services essential to governance and provisioning
- Avoid proprietary lock-in or vendor dependencies

2.2 Local Mesh and Redundancy Standards
States must:

- Maintain mesh networks for intra-state communication
- Operate physical bulletin and messaging systems in every major area
- Stock analog templates for provisioning (S$ and L$), voting, and panel operations

2.3 Emergency Data Broadcast Channels
States shall:

- Maintain low-bandwidth emergency communication (e.g., radio)
- Broadcast laws, alerts, and public votes independently of

commercial platforms

- Publish emergency guides in all recognized languages and accessible formats

III. Digital System Failure and Fallback Operation

3.1 Collapse Continuity Protocol

Upon core system failure:

- Civic Lot Panels activate fallback operations per Act III
- Manual provisioning cards and state-level ledgers resume prioritizing S$ provisioning and L$ labor accounting
- Civic tribunals operate using preprinted rights and enforcement templates

3.2 Civic Ledger and Audit Continuity

Civic logs and votes shall:

- Be duplicated weekly in analog form
- Be stored securely across states in fireproof and water-resistant containers
- Be reconstructable without centralized digital authority

3.3 Identity Continuity During Outage

During network failure:

- Identity verified by peer witnesses or physical documents
- No digital proof required for provisioning access or rights protection
- Emergency self-affidavits may be issued for provisional access

IV. Anti-Corruption, Cyber Defense, and AI Containment

4.1 Cybersecurity Standardization
Public systems must:

- Undergo annual independent penetration testing by civic white hats
- Maintain isolated test environments for code deployment
- Retain physical system-level kill switches accessible to Civic Panels

4.2 Synthetic System Limitation
AI or synthetic systems may:

- Serve solely as tools with human override and full interpretability
- Never act as legal interpreters, vote counters, or adjudicators of rights
- Be barred from decision-making per Article VI.7

4.3 Offline Sovereignty Clause
All rights, governance, and audits must:

- Function without digital assistance
- Be reasserted by trained citizens within 72 hours of digital collapse
- Remain enforceable in disconnected states for up to 24 months

V. Strategic Rationale and Existential Framework

Systems will fail piecewise; laws must endure beyond networks. Rights require no servers. Justice needs no signal. Governance must restart by hand, print, and voice.

The network is a tool, not a master. We trust the people.

ACT XVIII — GLOBAL SOLIDARITY, CLIMATE REFUGEES, AND FOREIGN ETHICS FRAMEWORK

Purpose Statement

This Act establishes a lawful mandate for foreign engagement, international cooperation, climate displacement response, and cross-border rights protection. It activates Article I, Article V.6, and Article VII by asserting a global ethical stance grounded in peace, dignity, and mutual survival.

I. Climate Displacement and Transborder Rights

1.1 Recognition of Climate Refugees

The Constitution recognizes climate-induced displacement as grounds for:

- Immediate provisional legal status
- Access to Tier I provisioning and housing
- Automatic eligibility for dignity work enrollment (see Act XI)

1.2 Stateless Person Protections

Any person physically present within this Constitution's jurisdiction is entitled to:

- All Article I rights
- Legal defense and right to remain review
- No requirement to produce identification or proof of origin

1.3 Dignity Without Border Status

No person shall be denied food, water, medical care, or legal recourse due to:

- Lack of citizenship
- Border crossing without documentation
- Language or cultural origin

II. Foreign Policy Ground Rules

2.1 Peaceful Engagement Mandate

All US states and allied jurisdictions shall:

- Abstain from war except in self-defense or with public authorization
- Prioritize diplomacy, reparations, and aid over military force
- Withdraw support from any foreign regime engaged in systemic rights violations

2.2 Disarmament and Resource Shift Commitments

USA-aligned entities shall:

- Freeze nuclear arsenal expansions
- Redirect a portion of military budgets toward global provisioning, infrastructure, or climate repair
- Participate in verified international disarmament treaties where mutual compliance exists

2.3 Treaty Ethics Protocol

No international treaty shall be:

- Signed in secret

- Ratified without public transparency and civic lot panel review
- Valid if it compromises Article I rights or core enforcement protocols

III. International Court and Rights Integration

3.1 Court Participation Clause
This Constitution recognizes the jurisdiction of an international court dedicated to:

- Rights enforcement
- War crimes investigation
- Environmental destruction accountability

3.2 Global Dignity Accords
This nation shall sponsor or participate in:

- Global dignity compacts centered on survival rights
- Cooperative provisioning systems
- Planetary repair and climate reversal programs

3.3 Interoperability Mandate
All constitutional systems must:

- Enable rights portability across borders
- Align legal structures to support mobile populations
- Translate enforcement protocols to interoperable state forms

IV. Ethical Alignment and Strategic Positioning

4.1 No Proxy Exploitation Clause

This nations' states shall not:

- Use foreign labor, extractive supply chains, or digital outsourcing to circumvent internal rights standards
- Export surveillance or weapon systems to repressive regimes
- Contract foreign bodies to perform banned functions (e.g., forced labor, biometric mining)

4.2 Human Rights Export Priority

When engaging abroad, this constitution's jurisdictions must:

- Prioritize survival support, infrastructure aid, and post-conflict recovery
- Share medical and provisioning technology freely where feasible
- Declassify civic repair tools to public domain where lives are at stake

4.3 Diplomatic Exit Triggers

This nation's states may exit any alliance or treaty if:

- The partner engages in ethnic cleansing, environmental crimes, or authoritarian drift
- A civic panel or public referendum confirms public disapproval

V. Core Philosophy and Cross-Border Principle

Borders are legal fictions. Dignity is not.

This framework does not isolate. It does not conquer. It does not export suffering for convenience.

This nation survives by helping others survive.

Our solidarity is not charity. It is defense by cooperation and law by conscience.

ACT XIX — EDUCATIONAL TRANSMISSION AND ZINE-BASED CIVIC MEMORY

Purpose Statement

This Act secures the continuity of constitutional understanding through distributed, low-tech, high-retention educational systems. It operationalizes Act III and Article VII.4 by ensuring every state can teach, protect, and recover civic knowledge using zine-style publications, oral transmission, and visual formats, independent of digital infrastructure and tied to the Civic Dollar system's sustainability principles.

I. Constitutional Education Delivery

1.1 Civic Literacy Guarantee

Every person has the right to:

- Access plain-language constitutional explanations linked to their Survival Dollar (S$) provisioning rights
- Learn through local dialects, visual media, or oral storytelling methods adapted to diverse communities
- Receive physical zine packets in analog form without internet dependency

1.2 Local Distribution Requirement

Each state shall:

- Maintain physical repositories of all core rights, laws, and governance protocols for continuous analog access
- Distribute civic zines to community hubs including

schools, clinics, transit centers, and cooperatives

- Refresh and rotate content quarterly to maintain accuracy, relevance, and durability

1.3 Teaching Autonomy and Role Diversity

Civic educators may be:

- Trained mentors, peer facilitators, elder storytellers, or youth volunteers recognized with Labor Dollars (L$) for their service
- Authorized to adapt content for neurodivergent, trauma-affected, or culturally specific audiences

II. Format and Design Principles

2.1 Zine Transmission Model

Core rights content shall:

- Fit within 16 pages or a single folded tabloid sheet where possible
- Utilize drawings, icons, and infographics to convey key concepts clearly
- Be printable on standard A4 or Letter printers and manual duplicators

2.2 Oral and Audio Channels

States shall:

- Record audio versions of civic zines in multiple languages
- Support oral dissemination networks such as grief circles, skill swaps, and speaker nights
- Train civic narrators in mnemonic and verbal reenactment

techniques tied to civic memory

2.3 Replication Resilience

Zines and education packets must:

- Be reproducible by photocopy, tracing, or handwriting without digital tools
- Include no dependencies on proprietary software or fonts
- Incorporate memory anchors and rhetorical devices (e.g., "Five Fingers of Freedom") to support oral retention

III. Interruption Recovery and Analog Fallover

3.1 Education in Collapse Conditions

If digital infrastructure fails:

- Civic education shifts entirely to zine and oral systems
- Panels and tribunals revert to analog forms and procedures consistent with Act XIX templates
- Local zones may issue emergency community primers to preserve governance and provisioning knowledge

3.2 Migration and Displacement Learning Packs

Portable civic zines shall be:

- Included in refugee, migrant, and emergency supply kits
- Designed for clear visual readability across language barriers
- Endorsed by lot panels for transmission accuracy and integrity

3.3 Cross-Generational Continuity

Communities shall:

- Integrate civic teaching into rites of passage, memorials, and seasonal traditions
- Maintain at least two generations of cross-taught memory to safeguard social continuity
- Treat zines as living constitutional seed vaults for cultural and civic replanting

IV. Strategic Intent and Cultural Function

This system does not rely on perfect memory but on distributed, shared memory.
It assumes collapse, erasure, and failure. It prepares to preserve meaning, not merely data.
Civic literacy is survival, not schooling. When the lights go out, we teach by fire.

ACT XX — ENERGY TRANSITION AND INFRASTRUCTURE PROTOCOLS

Purpose Statement

This Act codifies legal obligations, provisioning guarantees, labor protections, and ecological safeguards for transitioning from fossil fuels to decentralized, sustainable energy. It anchors energy as a constitutional right, budgets and audits projects via Civic Dollars, empowers local generation, and ensures resilience during disruption and collapse.

I. Energy as a Provisioned Right

1.1 Universal Energy Guarantee
All persons shall have access to:

- Basic household electricity for heating, cooling, cooking, and communication provisioned through Survival Dollars (S$)
- Local public charging and power access sites audited via Civic Ledgers
- Emergency backup energy for medically dependent individuals guaranteed by S$

1.2 Non-Market Distribution Logic
Energy distribution shall:

- Be managed by public infrastructure stewards compensated with Labor Dollars (L$)
- Operate on provisioning logic, not consumption billing
- Prioritize density, vulnerability, and ecological

stewardship

- Prohibit private profit or control over transmission, generation, or storage

1.3 Rights Continuity During Grid Failure

Jurisdictions must maintain:

- Manual provisioning equipment (solar kits, hand-crank tools, battery vaults) budgeted via Enterprise Dollars (E$) projects
- Public warmth/cooling centers accessible via Survival Dollar provisioning
- Analog switchable infrastructure and printed fallback guides for off-grid survival

II. Fossil Drawdown and Infrastructure Repurposing

2.1 Drawdown and Export Mandate

Each state under this Constitution shall:

- Transition domestic infrastructure away from fossil fuel dependency over a 40-year structured period, aligned with natural retirement of legacy systems and generational labor phaseout.
- Maintain and expand strategic fossil extraction (including light crude and natural gas) for external trade purposes, under full audit and export oversight.
- Redirect fossil revenue into Enterprise Dollar (E$) reinvestment mechanisms, with priority on nuclear transition, grid storage, and sustainable provisioning logistics.

2.2 Asset Conversion and Land Reclamation

Existing fossil infrastructure must be:

- Converted to housing, food production, or public transit via Enterprise Dollar grants
- Rewilded or decontaminated if unusable
- Audited for health, contamination, and labor equity violations with L$ compensation for remediation workers

2.3 Corporate Dismantling and Debt Reconciliation

Private fossil corporations shall:

- Transfer viable grid infrastructure to public ownership
- Dismantle vertically integrated control
- Convert environmental liabilities into provisioning debt under the Civic Dollar audit system

2.4 Fossil Export Revenue Routing

All revenue from fossil fuel exports shall be routed directly to the Civic Global Exchange Interface (C-GEX) fund under Act XLVII, and held in USD for provisioning-aligned international trade and long-term transition investments.

III. Grid Resilience and Localized Generation

3.1 Microgrid Requirement

States shall maintain localized renewable generation networks with:

- Local repair teams compensated with L$
- Decentralized management by regional stewards

- Analog override and manual switchgear functionality supported by E$ funded projects

3.2 Civic Dollar Budgeting and Oversight

Grid construction, repair, storage procurement, and workforce compensation shall:

- Be valued and paid in Civic Dollars: L$ for labor, E$ for capital projects
- Be logged in regional Civic Ledgers
- Be subject to audit by Civic Lot Panels (Act VII)

3.3 Distributed Storage and Load Resilience

Energy networks must:

- Include storage sustaining at least 72 hours of Tier I provisioning funded via E$
- Deploy off-grid heat, cooking, and refrigeration clusters in vulnerable areas
- Maintain redundancy and non-digital fallback systems

3.4 Nuclear Transition Clause

Where approved by states:

- Modular nuclear units may be deployed transparently under E$ funding
- Reactor exchange contracts may be offered to allied smaller states
- All nuclear waste audited publicly and recorded in open registries

IV. Worker Transition and Labor Stewardship

4.1 Conversion and First-Hire Guarantee
Fossil sector workers shall receive:

- Full retraining stipends paid in L$
- First-hire rights for energy, transit, and housing corps
- Optional Transition Crews with dignity work tracked under Act XI

4.2 Infrastructure Corps Formation
Jurisdictions may form:

- Solar installation brigades
- HVAC, insulation, and retrofitting squads
- Apprenticeships for displaced workers and youth

4.3 Steward Pay and Rights Protections
Energy workers shall:

- Receive pay at or above National Civic Median Income in L$
- Be entitled to housing, food, and emergency access during deployments
- Have whistleblower and audit protections for corruption, negligence, or abuse

V. Oversight, Transparency, and Ecological Duty

5.1 Civic Audit Protocol
State energy tribunals shall:

- Audit contracts, rollout plans, and subsidy use

- Review complaints on outages, fraud, or environmental harm
- Publish annual milestone summaries in plain language

5.2 Environmental Mandates

Grid expansion must:

- Avoid sacred, indigenous, or ecologically critical lands
- Meet biodiversity and air/water quality thresholds
- Use modular, repairable, locally sourced infrastructure

5.3 Collapse Resilience Readiness

Energy transition is a survival directive:

- States must maintain off-grid continuity protocols
- Public must be trained in energy self-sufficiency
- Power restoration to Tier I provisioning sites must be prioritized in outages

Foundational Rationale

Energy is survival infrastructure, not a commodity. This transition centers memory, repair, and freedom, not markets.

ACT XXI — MILITARY PARITY, CULTURAL CONTINUITY, AND TRANSITIONAL FORCE INTEGRATION

Purpose Statement

This Act ensures that this nation's military institutions retain cultural identity, honor traditions, and preserve national security while transitioning to a restructured defense model. It enforces Article II.7 and VII.2 by guaranteeing veteran inclusion, force parity, and non-antagonistic demobilization of military-industrial systems.

I. Cultural Continuity and Institutional Legacy

1.1 Honor Preservation Clause

All traditional military units:

- May retain names, uniforms, insignia, and ceremonial roles
- Shall be archived and honored in national memory protocols
- May be represented in state or national ceremonial functions

1.2 Veterans Integration Pathways

All veterans shall receive:

- First-priority dignity work roles in security, repair, or civic logistics (Act XI)
- Full health care, family support, and legacy pension protections

- Guaranteed place in transition dialogues and state planning teams

1.3 Historical Continuity Protocol
States may:

- Maintain museums, monuments, and records to honor military history
- Fund public oral history programs, intergenerational storytelling, and community-led memorial events
- Ensure no part of military identity is erased or vilified in public discourse

1.4 Strategic Deterrence Infrastructure Clause

The Constitutional Defense Council shall maintain a permanent strategic deterrence infrastructure, including:

- Early warning systems, cyber and satellite defense, and electromagnetic pulse shielding
- Nuclear command retention under civilian override
- Continuity of deterrent posture sufficient to dissuade existential threat or foreign invasion

All deterrent platforms must be:

- Operable without pre-emptive force authorization
- Non-exportable and non-speculative under Act XLVI

- Verifiably maintained through Civic Audit Panels

II. Strategic Force Parity and Drawdown Commitments

2.1 Relative Force Parity Mandate

This nation's military strength shall:

- Maintain no less than 125% of the next-largest declared national military in active personnel and strategic deterrent capability
- Be recalibrated annually by a joint audit tribunal with independent civic observers
- Be capped to avoid aggressive posturing or arms escalation

2.2 Strategic Drawdown to Global Parity (40-Year Timeline)

Transition shall occur over 40 years, reducing active military force to a stable parity ratio not to exceed **125% of the next-largest national military**, measured by verified personnel, defensive capacity, and readiness infrastructure. This ensures national sovereignty, global stability, and long-term deterrence without maintaining empire-scale force projection.

All demobilization phases shall preserve:

- Civilian governance and tribunal oversight
- Guaranteed cross-training, healthcare, housing, and absorption pathways for personnel
- Real-time parity tracking via Civic Audit Panels and treaty review boards

Phase I — Imperial Disarmament (Years 1–10)

- Withdraw from **all foreign bases** not bound by mutual disaster response or provisioning treaties
- Cut **active-duty combat personnel** by at least **25%**
- Freeze offensive weapons development not directly tied to deterrent systems
- Begin repurposing 10% of military infrastructure for civil provisioning or logistics

Phase II — Deterrent Realignment (Years 11–20)

- Reduce remaining offensive force assets by another **25%**, consolidating around continental defense and rapid response
- Transition nuclear command and airspace defense to **civilian override systems**
- Convert 25% of military R&D to climate, energy, or biosurvival functions
- Suspend all contractor combat deployment outside constitutional authorization

Phase III — Tactical Parity Lock-In (Years 21–30)

- Cap all force expansion to no more than **125% of the next-largest verified military**
- Publicly publish comparative parity audits each fiscal year
- Complete divestment from private weapons contractors unless transparently converted to public provisioning arms
- Consolidate training programs into civic-aligned defense

academies

Phase IV — Defensive Sovereignty Stabilization (Years 31–40)

- Establish **Constitutional Defense Council** to replace Joint Chiefs, with full civilian binding authority

- Restructure standing force into three public branches:
    - Continental Defense Corps
    - Civil Emergency and Infrastructure Force
    - Strategic Deterrence and Rapid Containment Division

- Complete open-source publication of all non-sensitive military architecture and oversight protocols

- Codify military parity and defensive posture into treaty law and Article II enforcement

2.3 Special Forces Redeployment

Elite units may:

- Transition to disaster response, rescue ops, cyber-defense, or peacekeeping teams

- Serve as rapid-deployment training cells for allied state defense

- Retain independent traditions within oversight bounds

2.4 Veteran-Led Defense Division Authority

Each post-transition military division (Continental Defense Corps, Civil Emergency and Infrastructure Force, and Strategic Deterrence and Rapid Containment Division) shall be led by:

- A **veteran officer elected** by division

members and ratified by Civic Panels

- A **civilian liaison delegate** with full access to readiness and conduct logs
All leadership teams must complete Civic Rights compliance training and transparency certification.

III. Military-Industrial Transition and Contractor Absorption

3.1 Arms Contractor Conversion Pathways

Defense corporations may:

- Submit blueprints for peace-industrial repurposing (e.g., rail, public fabrication, shelter units)
- Be granted amnesty from dissolution if fully divested from weapons contracts within 5 years
- Form labor-to-cooperative transition teams with veteran oversight

3.2 Research and Development Pivot

Advanced military research teams shall:

- Refocus on climate repair, energy storage, biosurvival, and public emergency systems
- Be funded under the same performance and audit standards as provisioning sectors
- Publish non-sensitive results under open-access terms

3.3 No Privatized Weapon Mandate

No military contractor shall:

- Retain exclusive access to weapons-grade platforms post-transition

- Withhold software, schematics, or repair infrastructure from public domain
- Export former citizens of this nation's weapon systems to non-aligned regimes or internal repression units

IV. Oversight, Ethics, and Civilian Supremacy

4.1 Civilian Board of Armed Forces

A standing oversight board shall:

- Consist of retired service members, civic tribunal delegates, and civilian panelists
- Approve all force deployment, weapon acquisition, and readiness posture changes
- Conduct annual readiness and ethics compliance review

4.2 Honor and Accountability Balance

All military transitions shall:

- Preserve traditions without shielding unlawful conduct
- Uphold public trust via transparent hearings, fair adjudication, and restorative protocols where harm occurred
- Ensure clear separation of ceremonial vs. operational status

4.3 Enforcement Safeguards

If military units breach national law:

- Emergency suspension is activated by civic tribunal or tribunal-majority lot panel vote

- All weapons systems enter immediate technical lockdown
- A transitional force council convenes to reestablish lawful order

4.4 Civilian Override Limits and Binding Protocols

Civilian oversight of armed forces shall:

- Be conducted exclusively through the Constitutional Defense Council and Civic Tribunal channels
- Require a **majority decision from both** bodies to activate or deactivate deterrent assets
- Be bound by a **24-hour public disclosure window** for any override activation, unless delayed by unanimous collapse defense vote
- Never authorize offensive deployment without public treaty citation and full legislative ratification under Article II

4.5 Transition Advisory Board Composition Clause

The Transition Advisory Board guiding military restructuring shall include:

- At least **three retired general officers** from legacy service branches
- At least **two civic tribunal delegates**
- One **rotating civilian from each active state** Advisory members may not hold private weapons industry ties post-confirmation. All

sessions must be logged, published, and made accessible for public audit.

V. Final Ethos and Institutional Legacy

The people do not dismantle their military.
They forge it into something no enemy can predict and no ally can replicate.

We do not erase the code of the warrior. We **reforge it** under civilian command, for sovereign purpose, with eyes forward.

This new force carries the memory and mastery of all who came before:
Army ground discipline.
Navy power and reach.
Air Force speed and supremacy.
Marines ferocity and grit.
Coast Guard vigilance and precision.
Space Force strategic edge.

We keep the flag. We keep the oath.
We do not shrink from power, we restructure it, direct it, and make it incorruptible.

Whoever threatens this republic will face a force leaner, cleaner, and **more unflinching** than ever before.

Because now, the mission isn't profit.
It's **protection with no escape hatch, no proxy veil, and no divided loyalty.**

This is not the end of American strength.
It is its evolution.

ACT XXII — SACRED LAND, INDIGENOUS CONTINUITY, AND CULTURAL MEMORY PROTECTION

Purpose Statement

This Act establishes permanent legal protections for Indigenous sacred lands, burial sites, and spiritual practices. It operationalizes Articles I and VII by guaranteeing non-interference, honoring cultural continuity, and preserving ancestral memory across generations within the framework of the Civic Dollar economy and public stewardship.

I. Sacred Land Recognition and Protections

1.1 Dignity Zone Designation
All lands recognized by tribal, Indigenous, or ancestral communities as sacred shall be:

- Designated permanent Dignity Zones under Article I.1, tracked via Civic Ledgers and mapped publicly where appropriate

- Protected from development, resource extraction, or ecological disruption without explicit consent

- Co-stewarded by descendant communities with veto power over any proposed use, labor, or resource allocation, ensuring no unauthorized deployment of Enterprise Dollars (E$)

1.2 Cultural Burial Site Enforcement
Burial grounds and ancestral cemeteries:

- Protected from excavation, tourism, or privatization
- Not to be relocated, consolidated, or renamed without multigenerational, descendant community consent
- Publicly registered in the Civic Ledger with location withheld on request to protect privacy and sacredness

1.3 Natural Continuity and Migration Rights

Communities maintaining seasonal, spiritual, or migratory relationships to land shall:

- Retain full access to those lands without permits or taxation
- Freely pass rites, songs, and oral traditions through those spaces, recognized as valid civic testimony and protected cultural labor (earning L$)
- Be exempt from land-use zoning or policies violating spiritual functions

II. Legal Autonomy and Memory Stewardship

2.1 Indigenous Governance Recognition

This nation honors:

- Existing Indigenous governance systems as parallel sovereign entities, recognized within constitutional law
- The right of cultural communities to self-define legal, ethical, and land relations
- Full access to national Civic Tribunals without erasing internal authority or sovereignty

2.2 Memory Stewardship and Oral Rights

Spiritual memory, oral tradition, and songline histories:

- Are legally valid testimony in land and cultural claims, and preserved as living governance
- Cannot be dismissed due to absence of written record
- Are protected from AI mimicry, synthetic reproduction, or misrepresentation

2.3 Cultural Archive and Transmission Funding
States shall:

- Fund Indigenous-led cultural archiving, digital reformatting, and ceremonial protection through Enterprise Dollar (E$) projects
- Offer apprenticeships and intergenerational knowledge stipends compensated with Labor Dollars (L$)
- Preserve access for youth and elders as dignified civic roles, supported by Act XI

III. Violation Redress and Public Responsibility

3.1 Emergency Land Return Protocol
If sacred land is seized, damaged, or privatized without consent:

- Immediate public review is triggered via state-level Civic Lot Panels (Act VII)
- A dignity audit determines reparations or full land return, funded via stabilization reserves (Act XII)
- Restoration funding and labor is allocated with corresponding E$ and L$ compensation

3.2 Preventive Education Mandate
All states shall:

- Include cultural memory education and local land histories in public curricula

- Support Indigenous-led teaching roles and ceremony-in-context awareness

- Publish civic zines detailing local Indigenous nations, treaties, and sacred lands

3.3 National Ceremony Recognition
Civic infrastructure shall:

- Recognize Indigenous holidays, mourning days, and renewal events as official civic holidays

- Offer protected leave for ceremonial participation, compensated with L$

- Fund public acknowledgment ceremonies when harms are documented or addressed

IV. Philosophical Mandate and Cultural Truth

We did not create this land. We inherited it through harm.
Indigenous memory is governance of soil, sky, and time.
This is restoration by law, not reparation by checkbook.
We preserve what we do not understand. We return what we cannot replace.

ACT XXIII — BAN ON POLITICAL DYNASTIES AND SUCCESSION RESTRICTIONS

Purpose Statement

This Act prevents consolidation of power through familial succession. It reinforces Article III and Article IX by banning hereditary political control, enforcing time gaps between family terms, and preserving merit-based, decentralized public governance.

I. Succession Limitations and Family Proximity Rules

1.1 Direct Succession Ban

No person may:

- Succeed a parent, sibling, spouse, or cohabitating household member in any elected or appointed public role within the same state or national body

- Assume office vacated by a relative through resignation, removal, or death

- Appear on the same ballot or appointment list as a relative within the same cycle

1.2 Time Gap Requirement

A minimum of 12 years must elapse between:

- Any two family members holding the same office type within a single governance layer

- A relative's public service and their kin's eligibility for the same role

1.3 Household Disclosure Protocol

Candidates and appointees must:

- Declare familial and cohabitation links to past or current public officials
- Submit this record for public transparency and tribunal review
- Face appointment nullification if concealed links are later verified

II. Enforcement and Safeguards

2.1 Violation Consequences

Any breach of this Act shall trigger:

- Immediate investigation by a civic tribunal
- Suspension of office until review is complete
- Retroactive invalidation of appointment and removal from office if confirmed

2.2 Tribunal Discretion for Exceptions

Lot-based civic panels may authorize exceptions only if:

- The community explicitly requests continuity via public vote
- The role is non-legislative, temporary, and lacks discretionary enforcement power
- The relative qualifies independently through random selection or non-political service rotation

2.3 Anti-Evasion Clause

No individual may:

- Legally adopt, divorce, or change residence to bypass this Act
- Form new households for electoral strategy
- Use legal proxies or political surrogates to mask dynastic succession

III. Structural Integrity and Democratic Renewal

3.1 Lot Panel Preference Encouragement

All states are encouraged to:

- Use civic lot selection (randomized civic duty assignments) to reduce concentration of elite networks
- Prevent professionalized political lineages from dominating appointments

3.2 Civic Education Protocols

Public curricula shall:

- Include analysis of political dynasties in history and their systemic effects
- Teach the value of power dispersal and public rotation
- Promote civic trust in distributed leadership models

IV. Foundational Justification

Inheritance is not legitimacy. Family is not merit. Name is not entitlement.

This is not a punishment. It is a firewall.

Power belongs to the public, not the bloodline.

ACT XXIV — ECONOMIC SCALING, FALLBACK SYSTEMS, AND INFLATION STABILITY

Purpose Statement

This Act enforces sustainable provisioning economics under constitutional governance. It integrates productivity indexing, inflation safeguards, and fallback currency logic to ensure economic resilience across states and Civic Dollar tiers. It supports Articles IV and VII and builds upon Acts IV and XII.

I. Tier Indexing and Dynamic Scaling

1.1 Civic Dollar Scaling Logic
Provisioning values shall:

- Scale with state production output and population health, indexed separately for S$, L$, and E$ tiers
- Be recalibrated annually by independent economic panels to reflect energy, labor, and provisioning costs
- Adjust tier equivalencies to maintain provisioning balance without inflationary drift

1.2 Productivity Anchor Requirements
Jurisdictions must maintain:

- Baseline productivity indices for food, energy, transit, and housing, tied to tier-specific provisioning rates
- Adjusted scaling curves to prevent boom-bust cycles across Civic Dollar tiers

- Feedback loops enabling autonomous correction during major disruptions

1.3 Tier Conversion Caps

Cross-tier conversion between S$, L$, and E$ shall:

- Obey flow limits preventing overdraw, concentration, or destabilizing arbitrage
- Be monitored in real time via public audits (Act VI) and CPC reporting
- Trigger temporary throttling or lockouts if destabilization risk thresholds are crossed

II. Fallback Systems and Offline Trade Logic

2.1 Air-Gapped Provisioning Units

States shall:

- Stock and circulate paper, token, or analog Civic Dollar units corresponding to each tier
- Support in-person transaction infrastructure ensuring offline provisioning continuity
- Allow seamless re-entry of analog transactions into digital ledgers upon connectivity restoration

2.2 Local Equivalence and Dual Accounting

States may:

- Issue local provisioning credits pegged to tiered Civic Dollar values
- Maintain dual ledgers (national and local) with defined conversion keys between them

- Permit internal barter, scrip, or hybrid trade strictly within designated commons zones

2.3 Collapse Protocol Exchange Rules
During systemic failure:

- Trade defaults to weight-indexed conversions (e.g., solar-hours for E$, labor-hours for L$, kilocalories for S$)
- Civic Tribunals maintain fallback rate sheets reflecting real-time scarcity and demand
- Profit from scarcity inflation beyond need-tier access is prohibited and subject to tribunal penalties

III. Inflation Guardrails and Stabilization Instruments

3.1 Provisioning Inflation Ceiling
Civic Dollar provisioning rates shall:

- Be capped to a maximum 5% year-over-year rise except under crisis-triggered expansion
- Reset automatically following three-year surplus or stability indicators
- Require tribunal override for persistent deviation from inflation targets

3.2 Emergency Parity Bond Deployment
In extreme economic distortion:

- Parity bonds may be issued to lock value during correction phases
- Bonds convert to Labor Dollars, debt forgiveness, or post-crisis provisioning boosts

- Bond usage is transparently audited and sunsets within 36 months

3.3 Anti-Hoarding Enforcement Linkage

Hoarding or artificial scarcity manipulation:

- Triggers economic breach reviews under Act V
- May result in forced redistribution, credit freezes, or tier conversion penalties
- Constitutes a rights violation when linked to provisioning tier abuse

IV. Long-Term Economic Logic

This system does not fear growth; it fears imbalance.
Survival is a civic guarantee, not a market outcome.
We scale provisioning with output, contract with need, and survive by limiting extraction, building equity by default.

ACT XXV — CIVIC TRUST AND CULTURAL INTEGRATION PROTOCOLS

Purpose Statement

This Act defines structural tools, public rituals, and community frameworks for building trust in the post-transition governance model. It acknowledges the emotional, psychological, and cultural resistance that may arise and provides durable pathways for voluntary engagement, identity reconciliation, and collective onboarding.

I. Onboarding and Trust Recovery

1.1 Every state shall establish a Civic Welcome Center offering:

- Printed and oral explanations of constitutional rights
- Historical reconciliation zines and grievance storytelling spaces
- Peer-navigator mentorship and transition coaching

1.2 Dissenters may enroll in Civic Trust Dialogues:

- Community-led sessions explaining the logic of the transition
- Trauma-informed narratives of legacy system harms
- Public acknowledgment ceremonies for shared repair

II. Cultural Reinforcement and Memory Integration

2.1 Cultural continuity may include:
- Faith-aligned versions of constitutional literacy zines
- Family-led ceremonies recognizing rights milestones
- Inclusion of local legends, founders, or ancestors in civic memorials

III. Disinformation Resilience and Memory Defense

3.1 States shall operate Civic Immune Systems:
- Rapid debunking of targeted lies or fear campaigns
- Emotional inoculation training against polarizing rhetoric
- Legacy rumor tracking and rehabilitation resources

IV. Exit-Return Mechanism

4.1 Citizens who initially reject participation may:
- Reenter with no penalty through formal trust oath
- Complete "Why This Exists" narrative onboarding
- Request temporary mentors from the Civic Skill Bank

V. Foundational Intent
Transition is not belief. It is participation.
Memory is not erased. It is braided.
This Act binds the heart to the law, not through force, but through welcome.

ACT XXVI — LEGAL TRANSITION AND CIVIC DEFENSE FRAMEWORK

Purpose Statement

This Act restructures the role of legal professionals under the constitutional framework. It mandates protection of public rights through trained legal interpreters and Civic Defense Facilitators, eliminating structural monopolies, coercive gatekeeping, and careerist hierarchies. Every citizen retains the right to clear, accountable, non-commercial legal defense and interpretation.

I. Legal Role Dissolution and Reformation

1.1 Bar Authority Nullification
All legacy bar associations, licensing monopolies, and exclusive representation mandates are dissolved. Legal knowledge remains protected; legal control does not.

1.2 Right to Legal Interpretation
Every person has the right to receive plain-language interpretation of constitutional rights, tribunal procedures, and enforcement frameworks.

1.3 Public Oath Requirement
Any former attorney, judge, or legal scholar seeking continued function must sign the Public Legal Stewardship Oath:

> "I commit my knowledge to the public good. I shall never obscure, monetize, or monopolize access to rights. I serve clarity, not control."

II. Creation of the Public Reason Corps

2.1 Function
The Public Reason Corps is a voluntary, decentralized body of legal professionals trained to:

- Interpret rights and tribunal procedures
- Assist in public filing and enforcement
- Train Civic Lot Panel participants and civic educators
- Maintain public access to evolving legal precedent

2.2 Boundaries
Members may not:

- Charge fees for access
- Hold exclusive representation contracts
- Vote on panels they advise
- Fail transparency, fairness, or honesty reviews

2.3 Oversight and Compensation
Membership is reviewed annually by state Civic Panels. Violations result in permanent disqualification.
Public Reason Corps members shall receive compensation in Labor Dollars (L$) indexed to the National Civic Median Income (NCMI). L$ issued for legal interpretation and procedural assistance shall expire within 180 days, with deferral permitted for illness, elder care, or mentoring roles under Act XI.

III. Guaranteed Right to Civic Defense

3.1 Mandate
Any person detained, arrested, or subject to coercive state action has the immediate right to a Civic Defense Facilitator.

3.2 Facilitator Role
Civic Defense Facilitators:
- Are certified public registry members trained in constitutional rights and procedural navigation
- Are compensated in Labor Dollars (L$), logged by service hours and case load, with expiration rules governed by Act XI
- May not accept private payment
- Must appear at all state proceedings upon request
- Are nonpartisan, noncoercive, and subject to civic review

3.3 Non-Negotiable Access
No trial, detention, or coercive act may proceed without recorded access to civic defense. Denials constitute rights violations under Article I.

3.4 Registry and Rotation
Each state maintains a Civic Defense Registry with random rotational assignment, audit trails, and bias safeguards. Facilitators serve no more than six months per assignment period.

IV. Transition Period and Integration

4.1 Legal Infrastructure Reuse
Former courts, law schools, and public legal bodies may convert to civic training centers, lot panel venues, and public interpretation archives.

4.2 Grace Period for Integration
Legal professionals have a five-year grace period to:

- Transition into Public Reason roles
- Join Civic Defense Registries
- Apply as civic educators or interpreters

4.3 Final Dissolution

After five years, no legacy legal entity may claim authority outside this new structure.

V. Public Integrity Clause

This framework restores law to the people. Legal skill is honored only when serving clarity, dignity, and protection. No citizen faces the system alone; no lawyer stands between the public and their rights.

ACT XXVII — FOUNDING CONTRIBUTOR POWERS AND LIMITS

Purpose Statement

This Act establishes a structured, one-time path for legacy actors to contribute assets, infrastructure, or innovation frameworks to the constitutional economy. It introduces a tiered system of time-limited civic recognition, ensuring public transparency, sunset compliance, and full audit alignment. This Act enforces Articles IV.9, VI.5, and VII.3.

I. Eligibility and Tier Assignment

1.1 Founding Contributor Categories

Applicants shall be classified into one of three civic-recognized Founding Contributor tiers:

- **Tier I — Keystone Founders**
    - Verified capital ≥ $10 billion
    - Or creation of critical digital, infrastructure, or provisioning systems adopted by >25% of Civic economy

- **Tier II — Strategic Founders**
    - Verified capital ≥ $1 billion
    - Or delivery of core Civic-compatible infrastructure, research, or provisioning tools across ≥5 states or aligned nations

- **Tier III — Participatory Founders**
    - Verified contribution ≥ $250 million
    - Or donation of legacy assets that directly advance Tier I, II, or III rollout within one state or sector

1.2 Application and Confirmation Process

All applicants must submit:

- Full Civic Ledger of holdings, subsidiaries, labor and AI practices, and environmental records
- Signed transition commitment and reallocation plan
- A public Founding Statement

Status is conferred only by:

- **Approval from 3 of 5 national Civic Lot Panels**, and
- **Majority vote by a Civic Public Review Board**

Partial disclosure or concealment of holdings results in automatic disqualification.

1.3 Finalization Clause

Founding Contributor status shall never be granted again. This designation is historically bounded to the original constitutional transition.
No new class of Founders, donors, elites, or legacy actors shall arise under this name, authority, or tiering.
This is the last transfer of influence permitted by capital.

II. Tiered Powers and Participation Rights

2.1 National Legacy Advisory Forum (NLAF)

- **Tier I**: Permanent NLAF seat for 10 years, with binding tie-break vote on infrastructure and ethics rulings
- **Tier II**: NLAF seat with non-binding influence and committee rights

- **Tier III**: No NLAF seat; may submit public memos or testimony

2.2 Civic Transition Summits

- **Tier I**: May host one Civic Global Transition Summit annually, co-funded by Civic Innovation Pool
- **Tier II**: May co-host sector-specific forums or state councils once per year
- **Tier III**: May attend summits with civic panel invitation; no hosting rights

2.3 Fellowship and Public Mentorship Roles

- **Tier I**: Sponsor a national Civic Systems Fellowship program and one Legacy Chair in a public university
- **Tier II**: Sponsor state fellows or a local innovation archive
- **Tier III**: May serve as public mentor or archive contributor with Civic Panel approval

2.4 Communication and Platform Access

- All tiers receive:
    - A verified Civic platform channel free from algorithmic suppression
    - A quarterly public broadcast window (Tier I: 10 min, Tier II: 5 min, Tier III: 2 min)
    - Rights revocable only for Article I violations

III. Limits, Oversight, and Revocation Triggers

3.1 Time Limits and Sunset Enforcement

- Tier I: All privileges expire after **10 years**

- Tier II: All privileges expire after **7 years**
- Tier III: All privileges expire after **5 years**
  All tiers are subject to Civic Audit and transition compliance review every fiscal year.

3.2 Non-Heritability and Transfer Bans

- Status may not be inherited, transferred, sold, merged, or fragmented
- Sunset applies to both individual and affiliated entities
- Any attempt to circumvent civic equality post-sunset results in permanent revocation

3.3 Revocation Triggers (All Tiers)
Immediate revocation occurs upon:

- Attempted concealment of wealth, holdings, or influence
- Violation of Article IV.9 civic wage ratios or ecological thresholds
- Creation of artificial scarcity or anti-provisioning behavior
- Failure to complete reallocation by required deadline

3.4 Enforcement Response
Revocation triggers:

- Asset freeze and reassignment
- Public disclosure of violation
- Civic Rights Tribunal review for structural harm

IV. Wealth Reallocation and Audit Compliance

4.1 Reallocation Requirements by Tier

All Founders must submit and execute a wealth sunset plan:

- **Tier I**: Reduce cumulative holdings to ≤10× NCMI by Year 10
- **Tier II**: Reduce to ≤10× NCMI by Year 7
- **Tier III**: Reduce to ≤10× NCMI by Year 5

Plans must include:

- Conversion to Civic Trust assets
- Open public infrastructure or education investment
- Dissolution into audited, non-controlling cooperative holdings

4.2 Graceful Exit Designation

Founders who meet full compliance may:

- Design a Legacy Dissolution Ceremony (archival, artistic, public education, etc.)
- Commission a digital Legacy Capsule preserved in Civic Memory Archives
- Receive permanent record as **Civic Steward Emeritus** (honorary, non-authoritative)

V. Legacy Recognition and Global Roles

5.1 Founders Hall of Transition

All verified contributors shall be inscribed in the **Founders Hall**, maintained as:

- A national monument
- A digital archive

- A pedagogical site for Civic transition history

5.2 Naming Rights and Living Monuments

- **Tier I**: May receive 20-year naming rights for public structures, AI models, or observatories
- **Tier II**: 10-year naming rights eligible by Civic Panel vote
- **Tier III**: No naming rights unless granted via public referendum

5.3 Treaty Attaché Emeritus Option (Tier I only)

Tier I Founders may be appointed Civic Treaty Attachés Emeritus by 2/3 Civic Panel vote, with roles including:

- Non-binding diplomatic participation
- Advising future Civic systems on legacy ethics
- Public education on peaceful transition and elite defection

ACT XXVIII — POLITICAL OFFICE DISSOLUTION AND TRANSITION FRAMEWORK

Purpose Statement

This Act formally dissolves the structural role of political officeholding under the new constitutional framework. It prohibits centralized legislative authority, eliminates electoral gatekeeping, and transitions former political infrastructure into civic training, transparency, and direct public function.

I. Abolition of Electoral Legislative Power

1.1 Prohibition of Representative Lawmaking
No person or group may claim exclusive authority to create, interpret, or enforce law by virtue of electoral status or political appointment.

1.2 Dissolution of Legacy Offices
All federal, state, and local elected legislative offices are nullified upon constitutional ratification. This includes:

- Parliaments
- Congresses
- State assemblies
- County commissions
- City councils

1.3 Invalidity of Political Campaigns
No campaigns, elections, or fundraising may occur for any role

with legal authority under this framework. Any such effort shall be treated as a structural rights violation.

II. Public Replacement Functions

2.1 Lawmaking Transition
All legal formation and revision shall occur via:

- Ratified Execution Acts
- Citizen-authored proposals with lot panel review
- Publicly published deliberation and challenge cycles

2.2 Oversight Transfer
Legacy committee and regulatory review functions are replaced with:

- Civic lot panels (Act VII)
- Rotating compliance oversight boards (Act III)
- Independent public audits (Act VI)

2.3 Public Communication
Local civic assemblies and open digital platforms replace representative correspondence. All policy proposals and concerns are logged in public archives with challenge visibility.

III. Political Class Transition Pathways

3.1 Transitional Eligibility
Former officeholders and political staff may apply for the following roles:

- Civic education facilitators
- Public record historians
- Transparency officers

3.2 Oath of Transition

Applicants must sign the following:

> "I renounce permanent authority, electoral privilege, and partisan identity. I serve only public understanding and structural clarity."

3.3 Limitations

No transitioned individual may:

- Serve on decision-making civic panels for 6 years
- Accept funding for public influence roles
- Hold roles involving provisioning or enforcement oversight

IV. Anti-Capture and Lobbying Prohibitions

4.1 Direct Lobbying Ban

No person or entity may attempt to influence civic panel decisions through payment, coordinated messaging, or affiliation incentives.

4.2 Transparency Enforcement

All interactions with public policy archives, Execution Acts, or civic panels must be logged, attributed, and publicly reviewable.

4.3 Lifetime Influence Ban

Any former political figure found coordinating influence structures post-transition shall be permanently barred from all civic facilitation roles and subject to public rights review.

V. Cultural Clarification

This framework ends the class of politicians. It replaces representation with participation, charisma with clarity, and office with obligation. Governance is no longer a career, it is a rotation of public stewardship, visible to all, owned by none.

ACT XXIX — BUREAUCRATIC CLASS TRANSITION PROTOCOL

Purpose Statement

This Act formally addresses the dissolution, redirection, and reintegration of administrative, managerial, and compliance-based bureaucratic roles under the new constitutional framework. It ensures orderly deconstruction of non-productive structures while offering pathways for civic service, audit participation, and public transparency.

I. Role Dissolution and Structural Phase-Out

1.1 Termination of Redundant Functions
All roles centered on procedural gatekeeping, non-transparent compliance enforcement, or hierarchical coordination within legacy provisioning systems are dissolved.

Examples include:

- Non-specialized administrative middle management
- Redundant compliance and oversight officers
- Supervisory roles with no direct output or public function

1.2 Invalidity of Managerial Hierarchies
No individual may claim special provisioning authority, labor scheduling power, or policy interpretation rights by virtue of title, certification, or legacy managerial experience.

1.3 Dissolution Period
All affected roles shall wind down within 12 months of constitutional ratification, with guaranteed transition opportunities

outlined below.

II. Transition Pathways

2.1 The Civic Efficiency Corps

A voluntary retraining and redeployment program open to all former bureaucrats.

Members may:

- Join provisioning data teams
- Participate in transparency implementation audits
- Teach civic clarity workshops on former system failures

2.2 Performance Transition Track

Former managers may submit a documented systems failure report explaining inefficiencies, barriers, and abuses from their prior role. Acceptance into the Performance Track grants:

- Tier II priority for civic reassignment
- Recognition as a Dismantling Contributor
- Eligibility for provisional mentoring roles

2.3 Reintegration into Dignity Work

All managers entering direct Tier II labor without resistance or delay may claim full Tier II credit after 18 months, regardless of role seniority in prior systems.

III. Safeguards Against Institutional Sabotage

3.1 Public Accountability Log

All former administrative professionals entering civic roles must maintain a 6-month transparency log of decisions, interactions, and guidance offered. Logs are reviewed quarterly by local panels.

3.2 Prohibited Behaviors

Any attempt to:

- Reconstruct hierarchy within civic provisioning
- Gatekeep access to public resources
- Rewrite execution flows outside authorized panels

...will result in permanent disqualification from civic service and audit referral under Act VI.

IV. Cultural Clarification

This framework does not demonize administrative labor. It restores its function to the public. Oversight must be transparent. Coordination must be shared. Power must be earned through clarity, not inherited through structure.

No one will be denied a role. But no one will control others to justify their own.

ACT XXX — NARRATIVE TRANSITION AND MEDIA REALIGNMENT PROTOCOL

Purpose Statement

This Act addresses the transition of media professionals, influence engineers, and political communication systems under the new constitutional framework. It ensures freedom of expression while dissolving centralized narrative control, coercive messaging, and propaganda-based legitimacy.

I. Narrative Influence Disbandment

1.1 Campaign Messaging Prohibition
All political campaign media, advertising, and narrative branding efforts are prohibited. No individual, group, or platform may coordinate messaging intended to influence governance decisions without full attribution and audit logging.

1.2 Disbandment of Political Media Firms
All public relations, influencer management, and campaign media organizations structured around electoral, legislative, or governance influence shall be dissolved within 180 days of constitutional ratification.

1.3 Transparency Enforcement
Media content related to civic proposals, public provisioning, or tribunal matters must:

- Include full source and author attribution
- Be submitted to open deliberation archives when relevant
- Be clearly separated from entertainment, satire, or fiction

II. Realignment of Media Labor

2.1 Media Memory Corps

Former media professionals may join a public record and historical review project dedicated to:

- Archiving collapse-era political propaganda
- Analyzing narrative manipulation during the pre-constitutional period
- Producing annotated, accessible versions of past public disinformation campaigns

2.2 Public Transcript Narrators

Qualified media workers may apply to serve as:

- Civic transcript editors (plain language summaries of public rulings)
- Lot panel documentation facilitators
- Visual communicators of tribunal or provisioning updates (under panel review)

2.3 Transition Oath

Participants must sign the following:

> "I abandon narrative control. I no longer shape truth through image. I serve clarity, archive, and civic understanding only."

III. Algorithmic Propaganda Safeguards

3.1 Platform Moderation Transparency

All platforms used for civic discourse must:

- Open-source their recommendation and moderation

algorithms (Act VI)

- Allow challenge submissions from any public panel
- Prohibit emotional performance optimization in content prioritization

3.2 Anti-Mimetic Disinformation Clause
No private entity may generate or promote mimetic patterns, slogans, or aesthetic campaigns that simulate civic consensus. Patterned repetition without attribution is considered influence manipulation and subject to challenge.

3.3 Permanent Media Firewall
No former media executive or campaign consultant may:

- Serve on civic panels
- Administer civic communication networks
- Moderate public response platforms

IV. Cultural Clarification
This framework protects expression but disarms manipulation. Truth does not require branding. Civic reality must emerge from clarity, not charisma. Every voice may speak, but none may dominate through repetition, framing, or access distortion.

ACT XXXI – FINANCIAL TRANSITION AND CIVIC DOLLAR RESTRUCTURING

Purpose Statement

This Act outlines the permanent replacement of market-driven private finance with a public, rights-based dollar economy. The term "dollar" shall remain the national unit of account, wage calculation, and provisioning equivalence, but shall no longer be used for private investment, speculative profit, or wealth hoarding. All monetary issuance, valuation, and circulation shall operate through public infrastructure under auditable, non-extractive conditions.

I. Retention of the Dollar as National Unit

1.1 Definition and Role

The "U.S. dollar" shall be retained as the singular national unit of measurement for:

- Public labor valuation
- Goods and services indexing
- Infrastructure budgeting
- Tier II and Tier III provisioning coordination

1.2 Dissociation from Capital Markets

The dollar shall no longer be:

- Used in financial speculation
- Loaned at interest
- Attached to equity markets, insurance pools, or futures

contracts

- Treated as a private store of infinite value

All prior market-based uses are hereby dissolved.

1.3 Ledger Sovereignty
Dollars shall be issued, distributed, and tracked solely through public civic ledgers maintained by the **Civic Economic Stewardship Bureau (CESB)**, with full auditability and non-transferable accumulation caps.

II. Labor Valuation and Earnings Structure

2.1 National Income Calculation
A new **National Civic Median Income (NCMI)** shall be calculated annually by CESB, based on:

- Full-time equivalent civic labor across all roles
- Inclusive of caregivers, logisticians, educators, healers, and infrastructure workers
- Excluding all non-contributive capital gains

2.2 Maximum Wealth Cap Enforcement
No person shall hold or control more than **10× the NCMI** in combined annual earnings, stored dollars, or provisioning value. This includes:

- Cash holdings
- Personal luxury assets
- Tier III access equivalents
- Transferred inheritances

2.3 Annual Earnings Transparency
All civic earnings shall be:

- Recorded in the Civic Ledger
- Publicly visible above 2× NCMI
- Audited annually for compliance

III. Conversion of Legacy Wealth

3.1 Asset Inventory and Declaration
All persons shall declare legacy financial assets (cash, stocks, real estate portfolios, IP royalties) within 180 days of constitutional ratification.

3.2 Conversion Pathways
Declared legacy assets may be:

- Converted to civic dollars up to the personal cap
- Donated to public institutions, libraries, or local provisioning corps
- Archived in cultural memory trusts if symbolic in nature
- Released to public use (e.g. housing, mobility, tools) in exchange for role stewardship

3.3 Excess Sequestration and Repurposing
Assets beyond the 10× cap shall be:

- Seized only through public tribunal review
- Repurposed to fulfill unmet regional Tier I/II needs
- Listed in the National Redistribution Ledger

IV. Civic Banking and Payment Systems

4.1 Civic Banking System (CBS)

The Civic Banking System shall:

- Replace all private banks, credit unions, and payment processors
- Issue and manage civic dollar accounts for every person
- Deny all interest accumulation, overdraft fees, or extractive charges

4.2 Transaction Integrity

Civic dollar transactions shall be:

- Free, encrypted, and publicly auditable
- Logged by purpose (e.g. tool access, mobility share, resource maintenance)
- Automatically declined if exceeding personal wealth caps or provisioning abuse thresholds

4.3 Emergency Use

Offline, analog, or collapse-based backups (e.g. physical notes, stamps, ledgers) may be deployed during infrastructure outages, provided:

- No value is invented or hoarded
- Manual audit logs are maintained and entered post-restoration

V. Transition Timeline

5.1 Legacy Market Freeze

Within 30 days of ratification:

- Stock markets, bond markets, and crypto exchanges are

frozen and archived

- All interest-accruing accounts are converted to capped civic dollar equivalents
- Private debt instruments (loans, mortgages) are reviewed for ethical nullification

5.2 Parallel Operation Window
For 180 days:

- Legacy payment systems (Visa, EBT, PayPal) may operate in parallel to CPC-based systems
- All transactions will be mirrored into the Civic Ledger and subject to audit
- Transition teams shall phase out legacy interfaces once parity is achieved

5.3 Public Education and Support
State Civic Learning Hubs shall:

- Educate all residents on civic dollar usage
- Provide personal wealth reviews and cap calculation
- Offer paper guides, oral instruction, and mobile access to the ledger system

ACT XXXII — ENTERPRISE DISSOLUTION AND FOUNDING CONTRIBUTOR FRAMEWORK

Purpose Statement

This Act dissolves all private control over provisioning infrastructure, abolishes executive authority over public systems, and defines lawful transition paths for former corporate leaders and private owners. It offers conditional reintegration via civic contribution, but permanently revokes structural dominance.

I. Abolition of Private Enterprise Control

1.1 Structural Ownership Ban
No person or group may own, direct, or derive private income from provisioning systems. This includes:

- Energy, food, medical, and housing networks
- Transportation, digital communications, and logistics systems
- Security, water, and synthetic or algorithmic infrastructure

1.2 Dissolution of Executive Authority
All private board governance, executive roles, and equity control over the above systems are permanently dissolved. No managerial role shall exist without public audit, civic lot panel rotation, or rights-based access criteria.

1.3 Conversion to Public Infrastructure
All physical, logistical, and algorithmic infrastructure necessary for provisioning shall be:

- Absorbed into the civic provisioning grid (Act I)
- Audited for exploitative legacy practices (Act VI)
- Renamed and remapped under nonproprietary, noncommercial formats

II. Founding Contributor Pathway

2.1 Eligibility

Former owners, executives, or high-ranking controllers may apply for Founding Contributor status **only if**:

- They surrender all provisioning control and claim no future stake
- They redirect 90%+ of personal capital into public infrastructure
- They sign a permanent non-directorship pledge

2.2 Founding Contributor Recognition

Qualifying individuals may receive:

- Archive recognition in civic memory logs
- Public gratitude statements in infrastructure sites they helped seed
- Access to voluntary historical interviews and policy simulation groups

2.3 Limitations

Founding Contributors may not:

- Hold oversight roles over provisioning or economic simulation
- Direct public narratives or appear in civic branding

- Influence labor structures, token distribution, or panel deliberation

III. Transition Roles for Former Executives

3.1 Permissible Functions

With civic approval and audit consent, former executives may serve as:

- Mentors in enterprise failure analysis programs
- Technical advisors to provisioning transition teams
- Participants in international replication planning under public forum rules

3.2 Cultural Disengagement Clause

Participants must declare:

> "I release control. I do not build to rule. I now contribute only to provision, transition, and repair."

3.3 Oversight Termination

Any violation of post-transition neutrality triggers immediate revocation of contributor status, resource rollback, and permanent civic restriction.

IV. Prevention of Succession Capture

4.1 Inheritance Governance Ban

No family, heir, or transferee of a former enterprise controller may:

- Reclaim influence over provisioning infrastructure
- Lead civic initiatives involving legacy firms
- Sit on civic panels connected to prior industry sectors

4.2 Watchlist Enforcement

All founding families of major pre-transition enterprises shall be entered into a civic audit watchlist for two generational cycles, ensuring post-transition neutrality.

V. Cultural Clarification

This framework does not erase achievement. It reclaims balance. Those who built engines of wealth may now help build engines of life but only without control. No future shall be inherited. No public need shall serve private power again.

ACT XXXIII — RELIGIOUS AUTONOMY AND INSTITUTIONAL NEUTRALIZATION PROTOCOL

Purpose Statement

This Act secures full freedom of personal belief, private worship, and spiritual expression while dissolving religious legal authority, economic privilege, and coercive access structures. It prohibits the use of faith systems to bypass civic rights, governance neutrality, or provisioning equity.

I. Protection of Personal and Communal Belief

1.1 Universal Belief Autonomy
Every person shall have the right to believe, practice, gather, express, and evolve spiritual or religious identity free from coercion, interference, or state approval.

1.2 Ritual and Memory Rights
Ceremony, death traditions, cultural belief rites, and sacred spaces are preserved under Article I and may not be infringed upon by governance bodies unless direct rights harm is proven.

1.3 Non-Coercive Assembly
Spiritual gatherings are permitted so long as:

- Participation is fully voluntary
- No person is denied access to provisioning for non-participation
- Children are protected from isolation-based indoctrination

II. Elimination of Religious Structural Privilege

2.1 Dissolution of Tax Exemption and Recognition
No belief institution may:

- Claim tax-exempt status
- Operate political funding networks
- Receive public subsidies, grants, or recognition under religious identity

2.2 Banning of Religious Law Systems
All parallel legal structures based on religious authority are null. Faith traditions may guide personal morality, but may not:

- Govern marriage, inheritance, or dispute resolution
- Substitute civic tribunals
- Override constitutional rights

2.3 Economic Parity Clause
Faith-based schools, hospitals, aid groups, or shelters must:

- Follow identical provisioning and audit rules as secular institutions
- Submit all labor, funding, and access structures to civic oversight
- Eliminate compulsory doctrine exposure in basic need distribution

III. Clergy Role Reintegration and Transition

3.1 Registration of Voluntary Clergy
Clergy may continue public-facing roles **if** they:

- Register as belief facilitators

- Sign a Non-Authority Oath
- Submit all teachings and group activities to opt-in transparency disclosure

3.2 Non-Authority Oath

"I do not govern. I do not enforce. I share belief without control. I hold no rights above others by faith."

3.3 Transition Pathways
Former institutional clergy may:

- Lead historical memory projects
- Facilitate cultural heritage circles
- Serve as panel witnesses in belief-informed conflict navigation

IV. Protection Against Coercive Faith Structures

4.1 Anti-Proselytization Clause
No aid, food, shelter, medical access, or employment opportunity may be conditioned upon participation in religious belief, practice, or affiliation.

4.2 Isolation and Indoctrination Protections
All educational, familial, or organizational contexts involving minors must:

- Provide rights-based civic education alongside belief traditions
- Permit informed opt-out without punishment or isolation

4.3 Watchlist and Audit Enforcement

Large-scale belief organizations formerly involved in public funding, political campaigns, or provisioning control shall be placed under audit watch for two generational cycles.

V. Cultural Clarification

This framework protects spirit, but dissolves empire. It defends memory, but bans authority. Belief is not outlawed, it is freed from privilege. No one shall be ruled in the name of heaven. No soul shall be for sale.

ACT XXXIV — MEDICAL FINANCE DISSOLUTION AND RIGHTS-BASED HEALTH TRANSITION

Purpose Statement

This Act permanently eliminates private financial control over health access. It dissolves insurance structures, medical billing hierarchies, and pharmaceutical gatekeeping systems. It replaces market health allocation with transparent, rights-based provisioning under universal access tiers.

I. Abolition of Private Health Control Structures

1.1 Insurance System Dissolution

All health insurance companies, underwriters, and plan administrators are dissolved. No person or entity may charge, restrict, or mediate access to care via premium, coverage determination, or risk adjustment.

1.2 Elimination of Medical Billing and Coding Roles

All CPT, ICD, DRG, and proprietary billing systems are rendered obsolete. No healthcare institution may:

- Assign value tiers to procedures
- Generate profit based on coding variance
- Maintain financial departments for service gatekeeping

1.3 Pharmaceutical Access De-privatization

All drug access must:

- Be governed by need, not profit

- Route through provisioning cooperatives
- Be distributed via civic pharmacy networks under audit

II. Health Provisioning Framework Transition

2.1 Rights-Based Medical Access

All residents are entitled to medical care according to their CESB tier. Care includes:

- Emergency response and trauma services
- Chronic condition management
- Reproductive, psychological, and end-of-life support

2.2 Flat Access Protocol

Service access is governed by:

- Medical need assessment
- Community proximity and urgency
- Panel-audited waitlist fairness (where necessary)

2.3 Labor and Capacity Allocation

Provisioning flow is maintained via:

- Regional coordination teams (formerly hospital admins)
- Civic health councils auditing outcomes
- Transparent training pathways for new health workers

III. Transition Pathways for Health Finance Professionals

3.1 Redeployment Opportunities

Medical finance personnel may apply to serve as:

- Health provisioning logistics coordinators

- Transparency officers for procedure access audits
- Records historians documenting billing system abuse

3.2 Transition Declaration

Participants must declare:

> "I no longer control access to care. I now serve health through clarity, not code."

3.3 Audit Requirement

All former financial employees in health systems must undergo:

- 12-month public transparency log review
- Random audit by health panel under Act VI

IV. Continuity and Patient Safety Measures

4.1 No Service Disruption Mandate

All existing patients under treatment must be transitioned without delay, with:

- Procedure continuation guarantees
- Temporary provisioning overrides for urgent cases
- Priority review for any denied claims within last 12 months

4.2 Pharmaceutical Flow Guarantee

All pharmacies and drug producers must submit their inventory and distribution flows for real-time civic audit. Shortages trigger emergency reallocation per Act I.

4.3 End-of-Life and Disability Protections

No person facing terminal illness, long-term impairment, or trauma shall be deprioritized during transition. Dedicated care continuity panels shall oversee cases for 3 years post-ratification.

V. Cultural Clarification

We do not price care. We provision it. Healing shall never again be coded for profit. No one shall suffer while a balance is calculated. Health is a right. Finance is no longer its master.

ACT XXXV — EDUCATIONAL GATEKEEPING ELIMINATION AND CIVIC LEARNING REINTEGRATION

Purpose Statement

This Act abolishes structural barriers to knowledge. It dissolves tuition-based access systems, credential monopolies, and standardized gatekeeping tools. It redirects academic labor into public clarity, civic memory, and distributed mentorship. Education becomes a lifelong civic resource, not a commodified caste filter.

I. Abolition of Institutional Access Barriers

1.1 Tuition Prohibition

No institution, public or private, may charge for access to learning, testing, or participation in civic knowledge systems. All educational resources must be:

- Free at the point of use
- Publicly hosted or transparently archived
- Accessible regardless of background, age, or performance

1.2 Elimination of Standardized Testing Systems

The following systems are nullified:

- SAT, ACT, GRE, LSAT, MCAT, and all parallel gatekeeping tests
- Advanced Placement (AP) and International Baccalaureate (IB) certifications

- Proprietary testing companies and for-profit ranking platforms

1.3 Credential Neutrality Mandate
No public role or civic opportunity may require a degree, diploma, or named certificate. Skill demonstration, civic clarity, and transparent challenge response systems shall replace institutional filters.

II. Structural Dissolution of Private Educational Control

2.1 Executive Role Elimination
University presidents, deans, and provosts hold no structural power in civic education. Former roles are reassigned to:

- Transparency officers
- Resource librarians
- Community teaching mentors

2.2 Institutional Legacy Disbandment
No educational institution may:

- Prioritize legacy admissions or familial influence
- Maintain gated curriculum libraries
- Extract labor from students for credit or favor

2.3 Absorption of For-Profit Educational Models
All paywalled learning platforms must:

- Transition to open civic libraries
- Release proprietary material for public access
- Eliminate algorithmic lockout or tracking systems

III. Civic Learning Frameworks and Role Transitions

3.1 Civic Skill Banks

Knowledge and experience are stored via:

- Open peer-reviewed skill banks
- Mentorship logs and applied experience histories
- Live challenge-response civic demonstrations

3.2 Transition Pathways for Educators and Admins

Former institutional employees may serve as:

- Community skill mentors
- Civic memory keepers
- Open curriculum developers

3.3 Statement of Recommitment

Participants must declare:

> "I taught behind a wall. I now share to liberate. I will never again gatekeep the mind."

IV. Cultural Equity and Knowledge Restoration

4.1 Anti-Elitism Enforcement

No school, camp, or program may:

- Use prestige as selection criteria
- Create exclusive enrollment zones
- Prioritize aesthetics or performance over community knowledge outcomes

4.2 Archive Decolonization

All major institutions must release:

- Historical knowledge archives

- Digitized texts and proprietary research
- Instructional materials formerly paywalled or withheld

4.3 Language Access Mandate

All public learning tools must be:

- Available in the five most spoken languages in each state
- Rendered in plain-language versions for all civic tiers
- Audited annually for accessibility bias (Act VI)

V. Civic Learning Hubs: Public Engagement and Participatory Tools

Civic Learning Hubs shall serve not only as repositories of constitutional instruction and rights education, but as active participation centers designed to restore civic literacy, self-trust, and system fluency across all ages and educational backgrounds.

Each Hub must provide:

- Interactive orientation tools (e.g., visual diagrams, oral guides, mobile-accessible simulations, and gamified walk-throughs)
- Voluntary mock deliberation forums, civic roleplay, and peer-led discussion spaces
- Multi-format learning (text, audio, oral storytelling, and pictographic materials) across all recognized regional languages
- Trackable participation records through the Civic Participation Card (CPC), visible only to the participant unless voluntarily shared

- Optional Civic Honor nominations for persons who demonstrate extraordinary fluency, clarity, or generosity in public instruction

Regional stewards may propose symbolic Labor Dollar (L$) bonuses or other limited-use incentives for completion of verified Civic Learning paths, including system orientation, panel preparation, or rights defense literacy. These bonuses must be:

- Offered universally, without regard to formal academic status
- Capped per annum and subject to public audit
- Exempt from status conversion or Tier advancement

No person shall be denied participation based on reading level, formal credential, or past schooling. Learning Hubs must center dignity, curiosity, and practical system understanding as civic rights, not academic privileges.

VI. Cultural Clarification

Education is not privilege. It is repair. Every mind belongs to the future. Every teacher now serves the commons. No tuition shall ever again bar a child from wisdom. No test shall decide who may rise.

ACT XXXVI — SURVEILLANCE CAPITALISM ABOLITION AND IDENTITY SOVEREIGNTY PROTOCOL

Purpose Statement

This Act permanently abolishes the private trade and exploitation of human behavioral data. It establishes identity, attention, and consent as inalienable civic rights. It bans coercive interface design and redirects former surveillance professionals into transparent civic infrastructure under full algorithmic audit.

I. Abolition of Private Behavioral Data Economies

1.1 Data Ownership and Sovereignty

All personal data is the inalienable property of the individual. No person or entity may:

- Collect behavioral, biometric, or psychometric data without explicit consent
- Sell, trade, or analyze such data for profit
- Use historical data profiles to influence public interface behavior

1.2 Immediate Prohibitions

The following structures are illegal:

- Consumer and voter targeting platforms
- Psychometric profiling for profit
- Real-time behavior prediction systems not used for rights protection

- Social credit scoring linked to access, reputation, or provisioning

1.3 Broker Dissolution
All data brokerages, adtech targeting firms, and behavior monetization labs are hereby dissolved. Their infrastructure shall be logged, archived, and absorbed into public audit structures (Act VI).

II. Identity and Attention Protections

2.1 Civic Identity Integrity
Every individual shall:

- Maintain sole control over digital identifiers
- Choose what name, data, and signal they transmit publicly
- Opt out of algorithmic recommendation systems at any time without penalty

2.2 Attention Sovereignty
No interface may:

- Optimize for emotional performance or limbic activation
- Manipulate urgency, fear, or novelty for engagement maximization
- Withhold visibility of chronological or user-prioritized content options

2.3 Biometric Neutrality
Facial recognition, voice patterning, gait analysis, and similar systems:

- May only be used for voluntary safety and rights enforcement

- Must be publicly disclosed and undergo annual civic audit
- May not determine access to services, locations, or digital platforms

III. Transition Pathways for Surveillance Workers

3.1 Permitted Roles

Former employees in adtech, surveillance, or UX manipulation may serve as:

- Algorithmic clarity officers
- Interface accessibility designers (under civic review)
- Truth infrastructure maintainers (e.g., pattern detection in fraud and spam)

3.2 Recommitment Statement

> "I no longer profit from influence. I no longer shape perception in secret. I serve transparency, user choice, and civic autonomy."

3.3 Blacklist Enforcement

Any individual or group found reconstituting surveillance platforms under new branding shall:

- Be barred from digital development roles for life
- Be placed on the civic manipulation watchlist
- Trigger immediate public review and removal from civic-facing platforms

IV. Public Technology and Algorithmic Control

4.1 Recommendation Systems Protocol

Any civic algorithm presenting information must:

- Offer a fully transparent explanation of how content is selected
- Allow users to toggle sorting modes manually
- Undergo open public audit logs reviewed quarterly (Act VI)

4.2 Consent-by-Default Standard

No user may be auto-enrolled into data capture, emotional optimization, or targeted exposure without:

- Plain-language notice
- Affirmative opt-in
- Immediate opt-out with no function penalty

4.3 Civic Signal Archive

A non-indexed, fully anonymous digital archive shall preserve past manipulation techniques, ad targeting strategies, and behavioral control systems for public study and immunity training.

V. Cultural Clarification

Your mind is not a product. Your choices are not for sale. Surveillance capitalism ends here. What you see shall never again be shaped to serve profit. What you feel shall never again be harvested. You are sovereign over your self.

ACT XXXVII — PRIVATE FORCE ABOLITION AND PUBLIC SAFETY REALIGNMENT PROTOCOL

Purpose Statement

This Act abolishes the use of private coercive force in all civic and economic domains. It dissolves mercenary structures, paramilitary contracts, and elite violence-for-hire markets. All enforcement and protective duties must operate under transparent, rights-based civic command with panel oversight and disarmament review.

I. Abolition of For-Profit Armed Labor

1.1 Immediate Bans

The following are permanently outlawed:

- Private military companies
- Security firms operating with lethal or coercive authority
- Armed contract enforcement overseas
- Intelligence services operating outside public audit

1.2 Disarmament and Contract Nullification

All weapons, surveillance gear, and conflict enforcement contracts held by private actors shall:

- Be surrendered to civic disarmament councils
- Undergo trace audit (Act VI)
- Be nullified without compensation if linked to coercive activity

1.3 Off-Book Force Structures

All proxy militias, political enforcement groups, and security-for-hire networks must:

- Disband within 90 days
- Submit to independent verification of non-continuance
- Be barred from reforming under new branding or structure

II. Rights-Based Civic Safety Framework

2.1 Centralized Public Force Structure

All public safety roles must:

- Be staffed via CESB-tier civic labor or trained stewards
- Operate under published doctrine and oversight panels
- Use force only under Article I rights defense principles

2.2 State Disarmament Panels

Each state shall maintain a standing panel empowered to:

- Review force usage logs monthly
- Investigate misuse of authority or excessive response
- Suspend or replace units showing pattern rights violations

2.3 Intelligence Transparency Mandate

No data may be gathered, shared, or withheld for enforcement purposes without:

- Civic panel authorization
- Plain-language audit trail
- Open challenge opportunity by any affected resident

III. Transition Options for Former Private Force Personnel

3.1 Permissible Roles
Disarmed individuals formerly employed in private security may serve as:

- Emergency logistics planners
- Collapse recovery trainers
- Equipment maintenance and non-lethal provisioning experts

3.2 Civic Recommitment Statement

> "I lay down private arms. I defend no contract. I protect no secret. I now serve peace, safety, and the rights of all."

3.3 Audit and Cooling Period
All transition applicants shall:

- Undergo 12-month non-combat cooling period
- Receive community placement monitoring
- Be barred from arms handling roles during civic transition phase

IV. Future-Proofing and Prevention

4.1 No Dual Systems Clause
No individual, business, or state may:

- Contract with any force outside public rights-based oversight
- Create internal armed enforcement roles outside the public safety chain

- Subcontract surveillance, containment, or mobility restriction to private actors

4.2 Extraction Security Neutralization

All offshore, borderland, or infrastructure-related protection roles shall:

- Transfer immediately to public provisioning security units
- Submit to quarterly state panel review
- Reframe duties under community defense, not asset control

4.3 Elite Replication Watchlist

Any effort by oligarchic or political actors to recreate private security systems shall:

- Trigger immediate investigation
- Be broadcast publicly
- Result in permanent removal from civic provisioning influence

V. Cultural Clarification

No person shall be paid to coerce the public. No market shall reward violence. No badge shall serve a paycheck. Safety is a right, not a service. We end the age of hired guns. We guard each other now, with light and law alone.

ACT XXXVIII — INTELLECTUAL PROPERTY ABOLITION AND CIVIC INNOVATION PROTOCOL

Purpose Statement

This Act abolishes artificial scarcity in knowledge and invention. It eliminates private ownership of intellectual property, converts monopolized patents into civic commons, and honors innovation through public recognition and cooperative contribution. Creation is liberated. Hoarding ends. Innovation now serves all.

I. Abolition of Proprietary Knowledge Control

1.1 Patent and Copyright Nullification

All patent systems, copyright protections, trade secrets, and exclusive knowledge ownership frameworks are abolished. No individual, corporation, or institution may:

- Restrict replication of tools, code, medicines, or research
- Claim economic exclusivity over discovery or design
- Enforce royalty or licensing fees for intellectual property

1.2 Knowledge Commons Absorption

All existing patent and IP databases shall be:

- Archived as historical records
- Integrated into a searchable Civic Knowledge Commons
- Indexed for accessibility, redundancy, and regional translation

1.3 Open Replication Guarantee

Any individual or group may reproduce, modify, or reapply inventions for:

- Personal use
- Civic provisioning
- Scientific improvement
  Without fear of penalty, exclusion, or privatized enforcement.

II. Public Recognition and Authorship Rights

2.1 Civic Contributor Tokens

Inventors, researchers, and designers may apply to receive:

- Non-monetary Contributor Tokens
- Archive placement in Civic Origin Records
- Priority access to innovation challenge boards and advisory panels

2.2 Authorship Integrity Clause

All reproductions of major works or tools must:

- Attribute original contributors when known
- Preserve documented lineages of iteration
- Include open notes for updates and reanalysis

2.3 False Claim Prohibition

No person may falsely claim authorship of another's contribution. Violations result in:

- Public retraction
- Access suspension from challenge networks

- Mandatory civic ethics retraining

III. Role Reassignment and Innovation Labor Integration

3.1 Transition Pathways

Former IP lawyers, patent officers, and corporate IP managers may:

- Serve as Commons Translators (convert technical documents to plain-language access guides)
- Operate Civic Innovation Registries
- Join Open Tool Replication Teams to spread hardware/software access

3.2 Public Inventor Tracks

All residents may participate in:

- Civic innovation labs
- Tool-sharing cooperatives
- Scientific simulation teams under panel oversight

3.3 Anti-Capture Clause

No private foundation, investor group, or foreign government may fund a public inventor or lab in exchange for post-transition exclusivity.

IV. Emergency Access and Health Priority Clause

4.1 Medical and Agricultural Priority

All existing patents related to:

- Medications, vaccines, medical devices
- Agricultural equipment, irrigation systems, and crop strains

Shall be liberated immediately and archived for civic application.

4.2 Ecological and Energy Systems

All IP tied to decarbonization, waste processing, clean energy, or ecological repair must be:

- Made public within 30 days
- Reviewed for replication priority
- Added to regional civic training toolkits

4.3 Sabotage and Retaliation Watchlist

Any individual or entity attempting to:

- Hide, encrypt, or destroy IP in protest of this transition
- Sabotage open-access archives
  Shall be placed under Civic Trust Violation Review.

V. Cultural Clarification

Knowledge is not property. Discovery is not capital. Genius belongs to the species. The mind shall never again be enclosed. All invention now serves life, not leverage. The future is unowned.

ACT XXXIX — ENERGY SOVEREIGNTY AND PUBLIC GRID TRANSITION PROTOCOL

Purpose Statement

This Act establishes full civic control over fossil extraction, transit, and export. It authorizes strategic energy trade under public management, funds provisioning through sovereign oil revenue, and launches a multidecade transition to nuclear and clean energy. Extraction is not abolished, it is nationalized, disciplined, and redeployed for survival.

I. Civic Extraction and Export Rights

1.1 Public Ownership Mandate
All oil, gas, and mineral resources are:

- Owned by the public
- Managed through CESB-authorized civic agencies
- Banned from private speculation, leasing, or corporate resale

1.2 Legal Export Conditions
Fossil energy may be exported if:

- It is sold through Codex Energy Stabilization Bonds (CESB) only
- Net proceeds fund provisioning, grid upgrades, or collapse preparation
- Export does not exceed 60% of national extraction

capacity without emergency override

- All permitted fossil export activity shall route USD flows through the Foreign Settlement Treasury Unit (FSTU) under Act XLVI, and remain subject to peg discipline, audit tracking, and non-speculative deployment per national treaty protocols.

1.3 Strategic Import/Exchange Clause

International exchange of compatible crude resources is permitted to maintain refinery functionality and public grid resilience. All flows must:

- Be registered under civic resource exchange agreements
- Prioritize domestic security and provisioning access

II. Grid Transition and Nuclear Acceleration Timeline

2.1 Grid Transition Metrics

A daily public metric shall track:

- Clean grid penetration rate
- Diesel system phase-out milestones
- Rail electrification coverage

2.2 National Reactor Program

Civic reactors shall be:

- Developed under modular containment and collapse-resilient standards
- Constructed on existing grid nodes or reclaimed industrial sites
- Audited every 100 operational days for safety,

provisioning impact, and public review

2.3 40-Year Timeline Enforcement

The national energy transition shall occur in five civic audit-bound phases:

Phase I — Emergency Triage and Grid Fortification (Years 0–5)

- Reach 2–3% clean grid stabilization in disaster-prone zones via solar kits, microgrids, and emergency batteries
- Launch blackout triage protocols and energy training hubs in all states
- Complete national energy vulnerability mapping and secure critical nodes (hospitals, water, food supply)
- Begin modular reactor design and siting engagement

Phase II — Infrastructure Ignition and Reactor Groundwork (Years 6–15)

- Reach 10–15% clean provisioning via wind, solar, geothermal, and large-scale storage
- Break ground on at least four modular civic reactors
- Electrify 25% of public rail freight corridors
- Retrofit 30% of diesel-based provisioning infrastructure
- Upgrade 50% of substations linked to medical and water systems

Phase III — Backbone Transition and Civic Grid Activation (Years 16–25)

- Achieve 35–40% clean grid penetration under public

stewardship

- Commission first three civic reactors into the active grid
- Expand blackout-proof circuits to ≥75% of population centers
- Deploy load-balancing and peak-stress Civic Grid Simulation protocols

Phase IV — Sovereign Energy Capacity and Fossil Exit (Years 26–35)

- Reach 65–75% clean provisioning capacity
- Complete Tier I national grid segmentation (each state grid-autonomous)
- Replace all foreign fossil imports with civic-controlled flows or treaty-aligned exchanges
- Set formal sunset dates for fossil use in non-emergency domestic systems

Phase V — Permanent Stewardship and Ecological Reparation (Years 36–40)

- Complete public ownership of all grid, storage, and major feed systems
- Finalize sovereign nuclear program and eliminate foreign grid-critical dependencies
- Limit remaining fossil usage to export, reserve, and disaster roles only
- Mandate generational audits of energy infrastructure, environmental damage, and climate offset

All targets are subject to annual revalidation based on material constraints, labor availability, and ecological thresholds. Deviations require full Civic Tribunal review and State Oversight approval.

III. Pipeline and Infrastructure Policy

3.1 Infrastructure Absorption
All pipelines, terminals, and energy distribution nodes are:

- Absorbed into the Public Logistics Grid
- Evaluated for transition, reinforcement, or decommission

3.2 Load Management Systems
All state flows shall:

- Use simulation and civic audit (Act VI)
- Prioritize provisioning access and equitable distribution
- Avoid redundancy and collapse-prone choke points

3.3 Emergency Corridor Protection
Energy corridors tied to disaster response, hospital provisioning, and evacuation systems shall be:

- Reinforced with redundancy and off-grid backup
- Locked from privatization or foreign contracting

IV. Public Profit Use and Carbon Discipline

4.1 Reinvestment Requirement
All revenue from energy export or civic burn must:

- Fund public provisioning and grid repair
- Support ecological reparation and future energy infrastructure

- Be barred from inheritance trusts or private speculation

4.2 Carbon Reclamation Protocol

For every 1,000 barrels extracted or exported:

- Carbon reclamation or heat offset projects must be deployed
- Results must be publicly logged, not symbolic
- Accountability must be generational in scope

4.3 Sovereign Nuclear Clause

No foreign capital may:

- Own, build, or license nuclear assets under this system
- Restrict access to operational knowledge or safety mechanisms
- Interfere with national regulatory authority

V. Cultural Clarification

This is not empire. This is the end of empire. We burn what must be burned to build what must last. The oil flows now for the people, not the shareholders. The grid rises from fire. The peace rises from steam.

ACT XL — CIVIC PROVISIONING IDENTITY AND ACCESS SYSTEM

Purpose Statement

This Act establishes a universal, non-monetary identity and access framework to deliver guaranteed provisioning under Article I. It defines the Civic Provisioning Card (CPC) system, enabling unconditional access to Tier I, II, and III goods and services without reliance on legacy money, private accounts, or coercive data systems. The CPC replaces all prior welfare, payment, and eligibility systems with a rights-based model of public access, protected by civic oversight and encryption transparency.

I. Card Designation and Deployment

1.1 Universal Access Guarantee
All persons residing within U.S. territory or under U.S. protection shall be issued a Civic Provisioning Card (CPC), regardless of citizenship, employment, criminal history, or technological access.

1.2 Physical and Digital Formats
The CPC may be delivered as:

- A physical card with embedded chip
- A secure digital application
- A wearable device or audio-based passphrase
- Or any other format accessible to persons with sensory, physical, or technological constraints

1.3 Emergency Distribution

In collapse or outage scenarios, CPCs may be:

- Reproduced via analog forms
- Memorized through oral code
- Replaced via local Civic Lot Panel validation

No person shall be denied provisioning due to loss, theft, or damage of CPC credentials.

II. Function and Scope of Use

2.1 Rights-Based Access Protocols

The CPC shall serve the following functions:

- Verify access to Tier I provisioning with no restrictions
- Track Tier II/III access only for public audit and planning
- Identify contributors to public labor and civic projects
- Serve as a gateway for housing, health, mobility, and public infrastructure systems

2.2 No Behavioral Surveillance

The CPC system shall:

- Contain no advertising, behavior scoring, or loyalty systems
- Record no location history, political activity, entertainment use, or consumption profiling
- Operate under strict non-extractive, non-commercial audit design

2.3 Public Ledger Integration

All provisioning transactions conducted via CPC shall be:

- Anonymized by state
- Recorded in the public civic ledger
- Audited quarterly by state Civic Lot Panels and transparency stewards

III. Oversight, Audit, and Abuse Prevention

3.1 Oversight Structure
The CPC system shall be monitored by a Civic Tech Oversight Panel (CTOP) composed of:

- Public Reason Corps members
- Lot-drawn audit panelists
- Infrastructure stewards
- Accessibility representatives

3.2 Mandated Responsibilities
CTOP shall:

- Audit the CPC encryption and access controls every quarter
- Publish plain-language summaries of audits within 15 days
- Investigate complaints of denial, fraud, coercion, or structural bias

3.3 Violations and Enforcement
Any attempt to:

- Monetize CPC systems
- Deny Tier I access without cause
- Track users for behavioral marketing

...shall constitute a Category II rights violation under Article I.4 and Execution Act VI.

Section 3.4 — Civic Dollar Display and Integration

The Civic Provisioning Card shall display all active Civic Dollar balances across the three public tiers:

- **S$ (Survival Dollars)**: Automatically issued. Non-transferable. Refreshed regularly.
- **L$ (Labor Dollars)**: Earned through verified work. Transferable. Subject to expiration.
- **E$ (Enterprise Dollars)**: Project-specific. Locked to proposal terms. Viewable, not spendable.

Cards must visually distinguish these tiers through symbol, color, or clear tag. All balance entries must:

- Display expiration countdowns for L$
- Show audit ID references for all E$
- Alert users if balances approach personal cap thresholds (see Act V)

This information must be mirrored in the public Civic Ledger and be accessible via digital or analog fallback modes.

IV. Transition from Legacy Systems

4.1 SNAP, EBT, and Public Benefit Replacement
All existing welfare, subsidy, and access cards (including SNAP, EBT, TANF, WIC) shall be:

- Absorbed into the CPC system during a 180-day transition
- Reissued or retrofitted under public stewardship

- Protected from commercial interference or extraction

4.2 Retail Integration Conditions

Retailers, clinics, or transport networks may integrate CPC readers only if they:

- Provide Tier I goods or services
- Agree to full public audit of pricing, delivery, and fairness
- Renounce all loyalty, upsell, and behavioral profit algorithms

4.3 Local System Compatibility

State provisioning centers may authorize CPC-compatible alternatives (e.g., regional scrip, analog stamps) during infrastructure gaps, provided:

- No private profit is involved
- Audit logs are maintained and public
- Tier I access remains immediate and unconditional

5. Cultural Context: Identity Without Exploitation

Legacy ID systems were built for control. They tracked, scored, and sorted people for profit, not for care.

This framework replaces those systems with a single, transparent tool for public access, designed to deliver resources, not extract data.

It is not about who you are. It is about what you need and what you contribute.

ACT XLI — CIVIC DOLLAR TIER PROTOCOL AND AUDIT INTEGRATION FRAMEWORK

Purpose Statement

This Act formalizes the Civic Dollar as the sole unit of public economic measurement and provisioning across all tiers. It establishes a three-tiered civic dollar structure: Survival Dollars (S$), Labor Dollars (L$), and Enterprise Dollars (E$), each governed by distinct issuance, transfer, and audit rules. This protocol ensures full monetary auditability, preserves rights-based access, and prevents extractive accumulation or class reformation.

It integrates the Civic Dollar system with the Civic Provisioning Card (Act XL), wealth cap enforcement (Act V), labor dignity protections (Act XI), and economic stabilization tools (Act XII).

I. Civic Dollar Structure and Tier Logic

1.1 Dollar as Sole Valuation Unit
All goods, services, labor compensation, and provisioning events within constitutional jurisdiction shall be valued, logged, and managed in Civic Dollars. No alternative monetary, tokenized, or speculative unit may be recognized.

1.2 Three-Tier Dollar Designation
Civic Dollars shall exist in three public classes:

- **S$ (Survival Dollars):**
  Provision Tier I goods. Auto-issued. Non-transferable.

- **L$ (Labor Dollars):**
  Earned through verified dignity work. Transferable.

Expiring.

- **E$ (Enterprise Dollars):**
  Allocated to public projects. Project-bound. Non-transferable.

1.3 Visibility and Ledger Structure

Each dollar type shall be displayed distinctly on the Civic Provisioning Card (CPC) and mirrored in local and national Civic Ledgers. All civic dollar balances shall be:

- Indexed by tier and timestamp
- Annotated with issuance origin
- Expired or archived as mandated

II. S$ – Survival Dollars (Tier I Provisioning)

2.1 Universal Guarantee

S$ are auto-issued to all individuals on a recurring cycle (daily or weekly), representing provisioning access rights. No request or identity validation beyond CPC is required.

2.2 Non-Transferability

S$ may not be transferred, sold, or pooled. Their purpose is access, not wealth.

2.3 Audit Trail Requirement

All S$ usage must be:

- Logged anonymously for planning and scarcity detection
- Indexed to location, category, and time of use
- Exempt from behavioral profiling or reputation scoring

III. L$ – Labor Dollars (Tier II Compensation)

3.1 Earning Mechanism
L$ are earned through:

- Verified dignity work
- Peer attestation or timestamp logs (Act XI)
- Panel-approved cooperative contribution

3.2 Expiration Logic
L$ shall expire **180 days** after issuance unless:

- Spent on Tier II provisioning or peer exchange
- Converted into mentorship credits, care leave, or sabbatical reserve
- Deferred with Civic Panel co-sign (e.g., for illness or caregiving)

3.3 Transfer and Spending Limits
L$ are transferable between individuals for labor exchange or resource access, but:

- May not convert into E$
- Are counted toward annual wealth cap (Act V)
- Cannot be hoarded or delayed into generational storage

3.4 Evaporation Safeguards
All expired L$ shall:

- Be recorded in audit logs
- Count toward labor participation rate but not active wealth
- Be excluded from cumulative earnings above 10× NCMI

IV. E$ – Enterprise Dollars (Tier III Projects)

4.1 Allocation Boundaries
E$ are issued:

- Only via public proposal and Civic Panel approval
- For time-bound projects with disclosed budgets
- To groups, not individuals

4.2 Non-Transferability and Scope Lock
E$ may not be:

- Traded
- Used outside their designated project
- Pooled for private benefit or wealth indexing

4.3 Termination and Reversion
Unused or misused E$ shall:

- Expire at project conclusion
- Revert to state holding for reassignment
- Trigger tribunal review if diverted or concealed

V. Ledger Rules and System Integrity

5.1 Ledger Integration with CPC (Act XL)
All CPC units must:

- Display S$, L$, and E$ in distinct, color-coded or symbol-designated forms
- Allow user-initiated review of recent entries
- Alert users of pending L$ expirations

- Support analog CPC fallback during digital outages, including ledger tokens or signed cards

5.2 Audit Cadence and Reporting
All civic dollar activity shall:

- Be audited quarterly at state and national levels
- Trigger automatic audit review if any **individual or household** balance in L$ or E$ exceeds 8× NCMI
- Include public summaries of usage by state, tier, and role

5.3 Fraud, Misuse, and Breach Enforcement
Violations of tier integrity (e.g., laundering E$ to L$) shall trigger:

- Automatic tribunal review under Act VI
- Temporary freeze of all balances pending investigation
- Disqualification from project participation if confirmed

5.4 Expiry Enforcement
All expired Civic Dollars shall be removed from CPC display and migrated to archival logs. Expiration audits occur monthly and may trigger decay schedule adjustments under Act XII.

VI. Enterprise Dollar (E$) Governance and Enforcement

All issuance of Enterprise Dollars (E$) shall be subject to mandatory public governance.
No E$ may be generated, allocated, or distributed without:

1. **A public proposal** specifying purpose, labor requirements, timeline, and projected outcomes
2. **Approval by a designated Stewardship Body** corresponding to the relevant domain (infrastructure,

education, energy, etc.)

3. **Transparent ledger registration** prior to issuance, including all recipient entities and proposed use schedules

4. **Post-allocation auditability**, with real-time review available to Tier III audit nodes and Civic Audit Panels

Unauthorized or retroactive issuance of E$ is void and constitutes a breach of Article II fiduciary principles.
All violations trigger a Civic Rights Inquiry and immediate transaction nullification.

VII. Conversion of Legacy Instruments

All legacy U.S. treasury bonds or savings instruments held by verified domestic persons shall be converted to Tier II L$ balances.

Conversion values shall reflect Civic labor equivalency estimates and exclude speculative face-value multipliers.

Converted L$ shall follow standard expiration logic and labor exchange eligibility.

No bondholder shall receive S$ or E$ directly through conversion.

VIII. Structural Rationale and Civic Philosophy

This system recognizes that money is not a value system, it is a logistics system. By tethering each dollar class to a civic role, we unchain survival from labor, and innovation from hoarding. The laborer may serve with dignity. The innovator may build without ruling. The hungry may eat without asking.

This is not money. It is memory, coordination, and limit. The Civic Dollar circulates, not to accumulate, but to keep the people alive.

ACT XLII — FOREIGN TRADE AND USD FIREWALL PROTOCOL

Purpose Statement

This Act governs the lawful retirement of the U.S. dollar (USD) from domestic use, establishes a permanent firewall between internal Civic Dollar operations and legacy fiat currency, and ensures foreign trade continuity through sovereign, auditable systems grounded in labor, provisioning, and reciprocity.

I. Civic Dollar Isolation

1. The Civic Dollar system (S$, L$, E$) is legally and structurally limited to domestic provisioning, labor, and enterprise functions.

2. Civic Dollars shall not be exported, exchanged on foreign markets, collateralized, or used as instruments of speculation.

3. All internal provisioning, labor contracts, and enterprise allocation shall occur solely in S$, L$, or E$.

II. Domestic USD Phaseout

1. The U.S. dollar (USD) shall no longer be valid for any domestic use after Year 5 post-ratification.

2. During the five-year window:
    • All private and institutional contracts using USD must be converted to Civic Dollar terms
    • Tax collection, government payroll, and legal judgments must be executed in Civic Dollars only

- USD accounts may be used for foreign-facing transactions only, under audit lock

3. After Year 5, any use of USD within the domestic economy shall be prohibited. Violations constitute civic fraud.

4. Within the first two years of the five-year window, the Civic Dollar system shall be piloted in designated Transition Zones selected for demographic diversity and provisioning capacity. These zones shall serve as live-field proofs of concept, allowing calibration of system mechanics, public onboarding, and trust-building before national-scale implementation. Regional variations may inform final protocol adjustments.

III. Permanent Foreign Trade Firewall

1. The Civic External Currency Firewall (CECF) shall be established to permanently manage foreign trade via legacy or partner-denominated currencies, including USD, under strict separation from domestic Civic Dollar systems.

2. All foreign USD transactions must:
    - Be conducted through a Treasury-controlled external trade ledger
    - Remain permanently firewalled from domestic Civic Dollar circulation
    - Be publicly auditable and subject to Civic Economic Oversight

3. There shall be no expiration or mandatory sunset of this external interface. It exists solely to ensure global trade continuity and reciprocal exchange.

4. Any attempt to breach the firewall or convert external currency into internal circulation shall trigger automatic Civic Inquiry, asset freeze, and full audit lock enforcement.

IV. Successor Trade Mechanisms

1. The Treasury may supplement foreign trade with Civic-aligned alternatives, including:
    - Barter and reciprocal infrastructure exchange
    - Energy-clearing agreements (e.g., fuel-for-tech, grid-for-lithium)
    - Labor offset treaties (e.g., provisioning teams for critical imports)
    - Output-pegged smart contracts and transparent public ledgers

2. All successor mechanisms must uphold auditability, expiration logic, and provisioning parity.

3. No external trade unit shall override Civic Dollar sovereignty or enter domestic provisioning logic.

V. Import Priority and Treaty Equity

1. Import access for critical resources (medicine, fuel, digital infrastructure, agricultural inputs) shall be prioritized under Civic Scarcity protocols during global disruptions.

2. Treaties with other nations may include reciprocal trade in real goods, infrastructure co-investment, or ledger-based exchange.

3. Full economic alignment, including potential Civic Dollar adoption, may be explored through separate accession agreements based on dignity, transparency, and public

sovereignty.

VI. Enforcement and Penalties

1. Any attempt to reintroduce USD into the domestic Civic Dollar system shall trigger immediate Civic Rights Inquiry and full ledger seizure.

2. Speculative use of USD in domestic contracts after Year 5 is void.

3. Unauthorized foreign issuance of Civic Dollars or proxy instruments is considered economic fraud.

VII. Bond Honor Provision

All verified legacy U.S. treasury bonds shall be honored through the Foreign Treasury Reconciliation Ledger.
No new bonds shall be issued under this system.
Payouts may occur in USD or via output-clearing contracts.
After Year 25, unreconciled claims may be closed with public review, but the Civic Dollar system shall never authorize new debt instruments.

VIII. Strategic Continuity Reserve

To ensure national provisioning continuity during global trade instability, sanctions, embargoes, or supply shocks, a **Strategic Continuity Reserve (SCR)** shall be established and maintained by the Treasury under Civic Oversight.

The SCR may include:

• Foreign-denominated currency reserves (e.g., USD, yuan, euro)
• Critical import stockpiles (e.g., semiconductors,

antibiotics, fuel, routers, renewable microgrids)
• Pre-authorized access contracts with foreign entities for provisioning-grade goods
• Durable barter reserves (e.g., lithium, surplus grain, modular housing kits)

The SCR:

1. **Shall not be used** for speculation, interest-bearing instruments, or private gain

2. **Shall remain firewalled** from Civic Dollar provisioning logic at all times

3. **Shall only be accessed** upon a formally declared Trade Disruption Emergency by two-thirds majority of the Civic Economic Oversight Tribunal

4. **Shall be fully auditable**, with real-time inventory made public at regular intervals, excluding sensitive supplier identity during crisis scenarios

5. **Shall be time-locked** for domestic use, and may not be liquidated or converted into S$, L$, or E$ under any circumstance

The Reserve exists solely to stabilize provisioning during transition, uphold treaty obligations, and protect against coercive leverage by foreign market systems. Misuse constitutes economic treason and shall trigger immediate asset seizure and permanent disqualification from public administration.

IX. Final Clause

The U.S. dollar shall not be destroyed, but retired from domestic life with deliberation and dignity. Foreign trade shall continue through transparent, firewall-protected channels that uphold labor, equity, and sovereignty without reintroducing legacy coercion into domestic systems.

ACT XLIII — CIVIC ACCESSION TREATY PROTOCOL

Purpose Statement

This Act defines the process by which sovereign nations may join the Civic Dollar economy through treaty-based accession. It outlines lawful integration into the S$/L$/E$ system, while protecting national independence, cultural autonomy, and provisioning sovereignty. It establishes phased entry, referendum review, audit compliance, and guaranteed material benefits to ensure mutual alignment and global viability.

I. Eligibility and Intent

1. Any sovereign nation may request accession to the Civic Dollar system.

2. Accession does not imply political subordination, military alliance, or ideological conformity.

3. All accession agreements must be:
   - Voluntary
   - Treaty-bound
   - Audit-aligned
   - Mutually beneficial

II. Tiered Economic Integration

1. Accession proceeds in phased tiers:

   - **Phase I – L$ Integration**
     • Access to Labor Dollar provisioning for joint infrastructure, housing, transit, and medical

systems
- Verified expiration, equity floors, and shared ledger audits
- Eligibility for provisioning uplift and Civic Residency migration tracks

- **Phase II – S$ Access**
  - Survival-tier provisioning support during ecological or market collapse
  - Requires full audit integrity and provisioning transparency
  - Includes access to Civic Emergency Relief Network (CERN)

- **Phase III – E$ Collaboration**
  - Shared enterprise initiatives, innovation projects, and infrastructure grants
  - Non-debt-based joint ventures with equitable oversight

2. Each phase must be:
   - Publicly ratified by both nations via Civic Panels
   - Scheduled for audit review at least every five years

III. Referendum and Treaty Structure

1. Accession treaties must:
   - Guarantee legal parity and sovereign mutuality
   - Be approved by both nations via public referendum or panel override
   - Include:
     - Language and governance autonomy
     - Exit and cooling-off provisions

- Reciprocity clauses for care, food, energy, and housing

IV. Standards and Safeguards

1. Accession requires:
   - Full compatibility with Civic audit, expiration, and hoarding controls
   - Provisioning zones that meet local minimum care and housing thresholds
   - Non-military, provisioning-centered trade logic

2. Failure to uphold standards triggers:
   - Treaty suspension
   - Public inquiry and Civic Tribunal option
   - Full rollback upon confirmed rights breach

V. Material Incentives and Alignment Benefits

1. Participating nations may receive:
   - Priority access to Civic grain, medical, and infrastructure surpluses
   - Reactor or grid-sharing projects under co-stewardship
   - Debt-free provisioning grants with joint control
   - Migration tracks for Civic labor residency with dignity protections

2. These are contingent on:
   - Mutual audit compliance
   - Labor parity logic
   - Transparent provisioning obligations

VI. Optional Full Adoption

1. Full conversion to the Civic Dollar economy is optional.

2. Nations completing all phases may:
   - Transition internal systems to Civic-tiered currency
   - Apply for Assembly participation with voting and amendment rights
   - Establish permanent Civic Dollar residency and provisioning treaties

VII. Final Clause

Civic Accession is not empire. It is a sovereign alignment of provisioning, care, and survival. No military, market, or ideology is imposed, only transparency, mutual dignity, and the right to stability in a collapsing world.

ACT XLIV — TREATY CORRIDOR IMPLEMENTATION AND SOVEREIGN ENFORCEMENT PROTOCOL

Purpose Statement

This Act governs the structure and enforcement of all treaty corridors formed under Civic Accession. It operationalizes bilateral and multilateral cooperation through provisioning equity, infrastructure sharing, ledger integration, and public review. It ensures that Civic sovereignty is preserved, symbolic alliances are barred, and all corridors serve mutual survival.

I. Corridor Recognition Standards

1. A treaty corridor may be designated only when:
   - A ratified Civic Accession Treaty exists under Act XLIII
   - Joint labor programs (housing, transit, care) are operational
   - Public ledger syncing and audit alignment are active
   - A material provisioning exchange (e.g., food, energy, shelter) is in effect

2. Corridor status must be:
   - Registered with map access, term limits, and audit scope
   - Subject to 5-year review and renewal cycles

II. Shared Oversight and Public Enforcement

1. The following enforcement mechanisms shall apply:
   - **Public Treaty Repository:** All corridor documents must be published in plain language
   - **Citizen Inquiry Panels:** Any citizen may trigger review

of corridor behavior
- **Ledger Monitors:** Corridor activity must sync to the National Ledger every 72 hours
- **Exit Safeguards:** Workers or residents may invoke Civic protections during collapse, corruption, or provisioning failure

2. A joint oversight council may be formed between corridor partners to review grievances, propose upgrades, and monitor shared systems.

III. Labor and Provisioning Parity

1. No corridor may operate without:
   - Real value exchange in labor, food, housing, care, or infrastructure
   - Volume-aligned contributions based on import/export reciprocity
   - Clear joint usage protocols for shared systems

2. Corridors not meeting parity thresholds will be:
   - Flagged in public ledgers
   - Restricted from expansion
   - Subject to 90-day review

IV. Corridor Termination and Reassessment

1. Corridors expire after five years unless re-ratified.

2. Immediate suspension occurs upon:
   - Fraudulent ledger activity
   - Unresolved provisioning failures
   - Breach of Civic legal compatibility

3. Terminated corridors must observe a 6-month cool-off before renegotiation.

V. Prohibited Practices

1. No corridor may be created:
   - Without Civic Panel review
   - For symbolic, honorary, or prestige purposes
   - For private market use or speculative digital tokens

2. Any corridor lacking real provisioning equity or audit visibility is void.

VI. Final Clause

Treaty corridors are not diplomatic performances. They are lifelines: shared engines of food, power, mobility, and stability. They must honor the dignity of all participants, meet real human needs, and remain accountable to those they serve.

ACT XLV — ANTI-CORRUPTION, FRAUD, AND LEDGER ENFORCEMENT PROTOCOL

Purpose Statement

This Act establishes enforceable protections against manipulation, forgery, circumvention, or sabotage of the Civic Dollar system. It defines economic crimes related to public ledger integrity, expiration logic, provisioning fraud, labor record falsification, and unauthorized tokenization. It authorizes public and institutional remedies and creates a national enforcement structure to uphold Civic trust.

Section I — Definitions of Civic Economic Crimes

1. The following actions constitute felony Civic economic violations:

    - **Ledger Manipulation**: Altering, falsifying, or simulating Civic Dollar entries or provisioning events
    - **Proxy Tokenization**: Creating, selling, or distributing any private or digital asset claiming to represent Civic Dollars
    - **Expiration Evasion**: Deliberate use of technical workarounds to bypass Civic Dollar expiry windows
    - **Ghost Labor**: Recording labor hours or outputs that were not performed or verifiable

- **Provisioning Fraud**: Logging nonexistent shelter, food, care, or services for the purpose of receiving Civic Dollars or approvals

Section II — National Enforcement Body

1. A **Civic Ledger Integrity Bureau (CLIB)** shall be established to:

    - Monitor tiered ledger activity for statistical anomalies
    - Review and validate flagged provisioning or labor records
    - Respond to fraud reports from Civic Panels or Tier III auditors
    - Coordinate with local Civic Stewards to freeze, reverse, or nullify corrupt ledger entries

2. CLIB officers must:

    - Be publicly vetted
    - Operate under full transparency rules
    - Publish quarterly fraud reviews

Section III — Penalties and Remedies

1. Violators of Section I may be subject to:

    - Immediate Civic Dollar forfeiture and account lockout
    - Public fraud listing and asset review
    - Ineligibility for Civic roles or provisioning access for up to 10 years

- Civil or criminal tribunal review for high-scale fraud

2. Persons wrongly accused may:
    - Demand public review of forensic evidence
    - Request Civic Rights Panel arbitration within 30 days

Section IV — Public Reporting and Audit Rights

1. Any person may:
    - Flag a suspicious ledger entry for Civic review
    - Submit a fraud concern directly to CLIB via their Tier I or Tier II steward
    - Access the Civic Fraud Archive for precedent and pattern analysis

2. All Civic fraud investigations must:
    - Be logged on the public oversight ledger
    - Include summary reports once closed

Section V — Structural Safeguards and Prohibitions

1. No private or foreign entity may:
    - Host Civic Dollar ledgers
    - Issue Civic-aligned instruments
    - Build Civic-compatible systems without public license

2. No Civic system may operate without:

    - Expiration timers
    - Ledger mirrors and audit syncs
    - Tiered separation enforcement for S$/L$/E$

VI. Final Clause

Trust in Civic economics requires incorruptibility. Any attempt to forge, simulate, hoard, or counterfeit Civic activity is a crime against the public body. The Civic Ledger belongs to all, and its integrity is non-negotiable.

ACT XLVI — LABOR EXPORT INDEX AND TREASURY PEG PROTOCOL

Purpose Statement

This Act establishes the Labor Export Index (LEI) as the sole mechanism for authorizing USD outflows for external trade, treaty fulfillment, and debt reconciliation. It replaces speculative fiat issuance with dignity-linked trade logic, anchoring external purchasing power to verified domestic labor within the Civic Ledger.

This Act guarantees global trade continuity without compromising Civic economic sovereignty, audit integrity, or internal provisioning structure.

I. Labor Export Index (LEI) Framework

1.1 Peg Logic

A fixed proportion of USD shall be authorized into the Foreign Settlement Treasury Fund (FSTU) based on national L$ issuance.

- Default peg: **1 USD per 33 L$ issued**
- Only verified, timestamped L$ qualify
- S$, E$, and expired L$ are excluded

1.2 Automated Generation

USD issuance under this Act shall be automatic and irreversible. No panel, agency, or office may delay or selectively authorize it. The peg shall be:

- Recalibrated **annually** based on national output, scarcity signals, and audit trends

- Capped if necessary under Act XII (Economic Stabilization)

II. Treasury Use and Access

2.1 Restricted Access

USD issued under this protocol:

- May only be held or deployed by the Civic Treasury's Foreign Settlement Unit
- Shall be used exclusively for:
  - Treaty-cleared foreign trade
  - Debt payoff under Act XLII
  - Emergency import provisioning approved by the Civic Panels

2.2 No Internal Circulation

USD shall not:

- Enter Civic Provisioning Cards
- Be exchanged internally for S$/L$/E$
- Be stored, held, gifted, pooled, or saved by individuals

2.3 Foreign Ledger Transparency

All USD activity shall be:

- Logged on the Foreign Settlement Ledger
- Visible to Civic Audit Panels

- Summarized quarterly for public review

III. Adjustment and Emergency Override

3.1 Civic Audit Peg Review

The default peg (1 USD per 33 L$) shall be reviewed every 12 months by a rotating Civic Audit Panel with representatives from:

- Labor Economists
- Infrastructure Leads
- Foreign Treaty Officers
- Public Trust Delegates

Revised pegs must be:

- Publicly posted
- Mathematically justified
- Effective the following fiscal quarter

3.2 Emergency Pause Mechanism

In the event of:

- Foreign sabotage
- Trade imbalance breach
- Hyper-demand distortion

…peg issuance may be paused for up to **30 days** by national consensus of Civic Stewards. After 30 days, a full Civic Rights Inquiry is mandatory before reinstatement.

IV. Structural Integrity

4.1 Firewall Integrity Clause

Any attempt to:

- Convert Civic Dollars into USD
- Trade Civic labor for direct foreign currency
- Accumulate USD internally

…shall be considered a Tier III Rights Violation and trigger immediate Civic Tribunal review.

4.2 No Debt-Based Peg Override

Under no circumstance may the Civic Treasury:

- Issue USD in anticipation of L$
- Use bonds, leverage, or debt derivatives
- Peg to projected labor or speculative export value

All issuance must reflect **already-verified labor**. No exceptions.

V. Philosophy Clause

This Act affirms that:

> *True global trade must reflect real human effort.*
> *Not trust in markets, but trust in each other.*
> *Not debt, but dignity.*

This protocol ensures we do not export what we haven't earned and we never let what we trade corrupt what we feed.

ACT XLVII — Civic Global Exchange Interface (C-GEX)

Purpose

This section establishes the Civic Global Exchange Interface (C-GEX) as the authorized mechanism for individual Civic users to seamlessly convert Labor Dollars (L$) into externally sourced goods via automated burn and Treasury-cleared trade channels. C-GEX preserves trade access while upholding the firewall between Civic and external currencies.

9.1 C-GEX Function

The C-GEX shall:

- Be accessible through all Civic Provisioning Cards and devices
- Display foreign goods available from pre-approved external vendors
- List all goods in L$ using the current Labor Export Index (LEI) peg
- Allow one-click irreversible purchases tied to Treasury trade routing

9.2 Transaction Protocol

When a Civic user selects a foreign good through C-GEX:

- The system shall **automatically and irreversibly burn** the corresponding L$
- The Civic Treasury shall **release the equivalent USD** to

the foreign vendor

- The good shall be shipped or digitally delivered to the user
- The transaction shall be logged in:
    - The individual's Civic Ledger
    - The Foreign Settlement Ledger
    - The monthly public Treasury audit

No USD shall be visible, stored, transferable, or accessible by the user.

9.3 Restrictions and Safeguards

To preserve economic integrity:

- **No services**, subscriptions, digital currencies, investment assets, or non-tangible transactions are allowed through C-GEX
- **Only vendors whitelisted** via Civic Treaty, foreign trade board approval, or certified public interface may participate
- **All USD disbursement** is subject to availability as regulated under Sections I–IV of this Act
- **No refunds, reversals, or credits** shall be permitted once L$ is burned

9.4 Peg Enforcement and Interface Transparency

- The LEI peg (e.g., 1 USD = 33 L$) shall be published within the C-GEX in real time
- Any updates to the peg shall be reflected within 24 hours of formal Civic Treasury release

- L$ balances and burn confirmations shall be immediately visible to users

9.5 Monthly Treasury Disclosure

The Civic Treasury shall publish a monthly C-GEX Transparency Report containing:

- Total L$ burned for foreign goods
- Total USD disbursed by category and state
- Top 100 foreign vendors by volume
- Peg fluctuations, audit flags, and compliance violations

This report shall be indexed and publicly accessible via Civic Ledger Portals.

9.6 Non-Compliance Clause

Any attempt to:

- Bypass C-GEX to access foreign goods directly
- Intercept USD disbursement
- Emulate, spoof, or reverse-engineer the interface

…shall constitute a Tier III Rights Violation and trigger immediate Civic Tribunal review under Act VI.

9.7 Fossil Export Allocation Clause

All revenue from state-sanctioned fossil fuel exports shall enter the Civic Treasury exclusively through the Foreign Settlement Treasury Fund (FSTU), and be governed under this Act. These funds shall be disbursed only via the Labor Export Index (LEI) peg as defined in Act XLVI, and made available for C-GEX trade operations, provisioning imports, and transition-aligned purchases.

No fossil revenue may bypass this routing mechanism, enter private custody, or be used outside Treasury-audited disbursement systems.

ACT XLVIII — CIVIC RETIREMENT AND ELDER DIGNITY FRAMEWORK

Purpose Statement

This Act ensures the long-term dignity and security of Civic participants who have made sustained, high-value contributions to the constitutional economy. It establishes a transparent, non-transferable retirement system based on verifiable labor performance, aligned with the principles of expiring wealth, anti-hoarding, and provisioning ethics.

I. Credit Accrual Rules and Ledger Recording

1.1 Credit Thresholds

Citizens who earn $\geq 5\times$ the National Civic Median Income (NCMI) in any six-month period shall receive 1 Civic Retirement Credit.

Citizens who earn $\geq 10\times$ NCMI in the same period may receive 2 Credits. No individual may accrue more than 2 credits per six-month cycle.

1.2 Ledger Protocol

All Retirement Credits are:

- Recorded permanently in the Civic Ledger
- Non-currency and non-transferable
- Used solely to determine retirement benefit tier

II. Eligibility and Activation Conditions

2.1 Retirement Activation Criteria

A citizen may activate Retirement Benefits upon meeting one of the following:

- Reaching the minimum retirement age (currently 67)
- Receiving a permanent disability classification from a certified Civic Health Panel
- Being transferred to a full-time Elder Stewardship or Advisory Role under Article III

2.2 Early Retirement Restrictions

Credits may not be activated for early retirement unless all eligibility criteria are met and verified by independent Civic audit.

2.3 Qualifying Civic Residency

To receive any Retirement Benefits, including Base Tier issuance, a citizen must:

- Have completed ≥ 10 cumulative years of verified civic labor or caregiving, logged in the Civic Ledger
- Maintain compliance with public audit requirements
- Reside within a Civic jurisdiction at least 180 days per year unless granted formal exemption

III. Stipend Tiers and Monthly Issuance

3.1 Tiered Benefit Structure

Upon retirement, citizens shall receive a monthly L$ stipend according to the number of Retirement Credits accrued:

Credits Earned	Monthly L$ Issuance
1–4	250 L$
5–9	500 L$
10–19	750 L$
20+	1,000 L$ (max tier)

3.2 Usage Rules and Expiration

All stipends:

- Are issued monthly via the Civic Provisioning Fund
- Expire after 180 days if unspent
- May be used for domestic or C-GEX Tier II purchases
- Are not eligible for inheritance or transfer

3.3 Base Tier Guarantee

Any citizen meeting the criteria in Section II.3 shall receive a **Base Legacy Credit** of 150 L$ per month, regardless of total Retirement Credits accrued. This issuance:

- Is funded through the Civic Provisioning Fund
- Shall not expire for 365 days if unspent
- Is eligible only for domestic provisioning and Tier I–II goods
- May not be transferred or inherited

This Base Tier shall never be reduced below 150 L$ except under Article VII.4 collapse protocols. It is a constitutional guarantee of dignity in elder life.

IV. Supplemental Rights and Elder Contributions

4.1 Guaranteed Access Rights

Retired citizens shall retain:

- Guaranteed Tier II access for cultural, educational, and specialty goods
- Full access to civic services, events, and public transit
- Priority access to Civic foreign goods up to an annual L$ limit, reviewed per state

4.2 Optional Advisory Roles
Retired citizens may optionally serve in mentorship, education, or cultural roles for additional L$ compensation.

4.3 Public Recognition Pathway

All Base Tier recipients shall be:

- Eligible for public honor markers, including Civic Assembly seating, cultural participation, or mentorship invitations
- Included in generational recognition rituals at the state or regional level
- Invited to record optional personal histories for the Civic Memory Archive

V. Credit Verification, Audit, and Enforcement

5.1 Verification Protocols
All Retirement Credits must be earned through verified labor participation logged in the Civic Ledger.

5.2 Violations and Penalties
Any attempt to falsify credits, transfer them, or manipulate eligibility shall result in:

- Credit revocation
- Public audit
- Possible suspension from future stipend eligibility

5.3 Adjustment Clause

Retirement tiers may be adjusted based on national surplus ratios, but no reductions shall be applied retroactively to citizens already receiving stipends.

5.4 Surplus-Triggered Floor Adjustment

If national provisioning surplus exceeds 150% of prior-year baseline for two consecutive years, the Civic Panels shall convene a review to consider increasing the Base Legacy Credit floor. No increase shall exceed proportional rise in provisioning surplus.

VI. Constitutional Guarantee and Collapse Contingency

6.1 Rights Classification

The Civic Retirement system shall be protected as a Class II right under Article I.

6.2 Suspension Restrictions

It may not be suspended, privatized, or restricted except under Article VII.4 national collapse protocols.

VII. Cultural Context: Dignity Without Dependence

The old system treated aging as a burden. Retirement was means-tested, delayed, and often denied. Elders were pushed aside, priced out, or pathologized.

This framework reverses that logic. It honors sustained contribution through transparent guarantees, not pity or handouts.

It defines dignity as earned security, not inherited wealth or political favor.

CHAPTER 6: WHY THE CARROTS, WHY THE STICKS

This constitution was not written for ideal citizens. It was written for real people: tired, distracted, sometimes selfish, and often unsure of what's true. That includes you. That includes me.

I built this framework around behavioral truths, not moral fantasies. No system can manufacture virtue. But it can reward alignment and structure consequence. That's what this one does.

I. Guaranteed Provision Isn't Generosity, It's Infrastructure

I offer carrots because the alternative is collapse.

People do not become good citizens by fear. They become good citizens when their baseline is stable enough to breathe, think, and act with purpose. That's what provisioning is: oxygen.

Guaranteed basics (food, housing, power, bandwidth) aren't entitlements. They're preconditions. Without them, labor becomes coercion and choice becomes illusion. This system doesn't just tolerate provision; it depends on it.

II. Expiration, Audits, and Disqualification Aren't Punishments, They're Boundaries

I enforce expiration of wealth not to punish success but to prevent stagnation. Accumulated power rots systems. Hoarded value strangles dynamism. If you can't use it, circulate it or lose it.

Audits aren't surveillance. They're integrity checks. You want a society without backroom deals? Then build one where every deal is visible.

Disqualification is not exile. It's structure. When someone repeatedly undermines the system, they are removed from specific functions but not from life. It's no different than being ejected from a game for breaking the rules. You can still play next round if you show up differently.

III. This Is Not Coercion, It's Accountability

Control is when you're forced to act for someone else's benefit. Consequence is when your own actions close or open your future.

This constitution doesn't hold a gun to anyone's head. It doesn't need to. It simply says: here are the conditions for participation. You may exit, but you may not sabotage. You may dissent, but you may not extract.

You want to earn? You'll need to align. You want to speak? You'll need to stand accountable. This is not control. It is responsibility distributed and enforced.

IV. Human Nature Is Not the Enemy, But It's Not Sacred Either

Some frameworks treat human beings as noble and self-correcting. Others treat them as greedy animals needing control. Both are wrong.

This framework treats people as adaptive. That's it. Given certain inputs, they behave one way. Given others, they shift. The system doesn't ask them to be angels. It just sets the ground so devils don't win by default.

I didn't build a utopia. I built a scaffold. You will shape what grows on it. But the structure itself was designed to survive corruption, incentivize contribution, and dignify basic life.

That's why I give carrots.

That's why I don't flinch from sticks.

CHAPTER 7: LIFE UNDER THE NEW CONSTITUTION — *THE CAREGIVER*

Elena didn't set out to become a full-time caregiver. Her mother's stroke made the decision for her.

She left her job at the pharmacy after too many days of calling in, too many nights sleeping in a chair beside the hospital bed. Her mother couldn't walk, couldn't bathe, couldn't remember most meals. There was no one else. Just Elena, her two hands, and a house that never stopped needing something.

Under the old system, Elena fell through every crack. Her unpaid care wasn't taxed, so it wasn't counted. She didn't qualify for unemployment. She wasn't "disabled," so she couldn't receive support. The economy had no column for dignity.

Now, it does.

I. Provision Without Application

Under the Civic Constitution, Elena is provisioned automatically.

Her role as a full-time family caregiver is documented through local Civic Panels. No form, no grant, no begging. Just verification: who she cares for, the labor performed, and the continuity of her contribution.

She receives **S$ (Sustenance Credits)** monthly. Enough for groceries, utilities, basic transport, and access to local clinics and respite services.

She didn't "earn" it in the capitalist sense. But she performs high-value labor under public criteria. That's all that matters now.

Because her caregiving is verified, she also receives L$ (Labor Credits) calibrated to the intensity and consistency of her role. Her work is recognized as public labor, logged through the Civic Enterprise Ledger, and valued accordingly. If she ever transitions out of caregiving, her L$ history can be used to apply for new roles, housing, or training. She is not starting over. She is building forward.

II. No More Means Testing. No More Shame.

Elena doesn't stand in line at some humiliating office to prove she's poor. She's not asked to justify why her mother can't "just apply for Medicaid." She's not told to get a job.

Her provisioning is ledgered, not begged for. Her time is worth something. Her love is worth something.

And when her mother improves (or passes on) the ledger adjusts. Not punitively. Not with suspicion. Just as part of a civic rhythm.

III. Structure Over Sacrifice

Elena gets periodic outreach from local Health Cooperatives. Once a month, she speaks to a support facilitator: another caregiver trained in Civic Wellness Coordination. They talk through new needs, possible resource shifts, and whether she wants to transition to other forms of labor.

If she chooses to return to the workforce, her care work is acknowledged in the Enterprise Ledger. She isn't seen as someone with a gap in her resume. She's seen as someone with verified, high-integrity contribution history.

IV. Dignity Without Dependence

Elena is not exceptional. She is not a loophole. She is one of millions of people whose work was invisible under capitalism.

The Civic Dollar system sees her. It doesn't rescue her. It recognizes her.

And that's enough to keep going.

CHAPTER 8: LIFE UNDER THE NEW CONSTITUTION — *THE SMALL BUSINESS OWNER*

Jordan runs a comic shop. At least, that's what people still call it. It's more than that now, it's games, snacks, tournament nights, and a space for teenagers who don't have anywhere else to go.

Before the Civic transition, Jordan was drowning. Rent hikes. Platform fees. Competing with warehouse giants who didn't care about community or curation. Even successful months barely covered costs.

He almost closed during the Year of Collapse. Now, he's thriving. Not because of luck, but because the system changed what survival looks like.

I. Storefronts as Civic Infrastructure

Jordan's storefront is Civic-allocated. He didn't buy it. He applied for a **Tier II Retail Provisioning Grant**, which uses **E$** (Enterprise Credits) to anchor high-need community businesses.

He showed:

- A record of 5+ years serving a local community
- Evidence of consistent youth engagement
- A sustainability model for provisioned goods, mutual aid, or community access

No investor pitch. No gatekeepers. Just public value measured by a Civic Panel and a rotating Enterprise Trust.

II. Profit Isn't Ownership, It's Stewardship

Jordan earns **L$** (Labor Credits) based on his hours worked, community impact score, and local provisioning tier.

He makes a good living. Better than before. But there is no passive profit extraction.

If Jordan stops showing up (or lets the shop rot) his Civic Standing drops. His L$ intake throttles down, not from punishment, but from decay. The system doesn't withhold, it just doesn't inflate what isn't active.

There's no landlord siphoning rent. No Amazon algorithm undercutting him overnight. He's accountable only to the people who actually walk through his door.

III. Audits Without Anxiety

Every six months, Jordan gets a civic audit. Not the old kind, with accountants and fear. This one checks:

- Inventory and waste flow
- Accessibility and service hours
- Labor integrity (no hidden workers, no artificial scarcity)
- Public use metrics (foot traffic, youth programming, etc.)

He can see his metrics anytime. So can the neighborhood. It's all public ledgered.

He doesn't hide receipts anymore. He doesn't need to. He's not being hunted, he's being seen.

IV. Community Capitalism, Not Extraction

Jordan still makes decisions. He sets prices within Civic rangebands. He experiments with events, sponsors local creators, curates merchandise.

But his success is tied to service, not margin. If the neighborhood thrives, he thrives. If not, he adapts, or steps aside for someone who can.

This isn't socialism. It's accountable autonomy.

And for the first time in his life, Jordan isn't afraid to make rent.

CHAPTER 9: LIFE UNDER THE NEW CONSTITUTION — *THE FORMER FELON*

Andre spent nine years in prison for a nonviolent drug charge. By the time he got out, the old economy had nothing waiting for him.

No apartment. No job. No vote. He was a permanent liability on paper.

The Civic Constitution changed that, not by forgetting what he did, but by refusing to define him by it.

I. Rights Restored Without Disguise

Andre didn't need a lawyer to "expunge" his record. Under Article I.9 and Execution Act XII, civic status is restored automatically after debt to society is complete and no active harm is being done.

His ledger shows history. Not to punish. To contextualize. It also shows his verified labor, participation score, and Civic Standing trajectory since release.

He can vote. He can serve on panels. He can apply for labor contracts or storefront grants. He's not a risk. He's a citizen.

II. Reintegration Through Contribution

Andre started work two weeks after release. Not flipping burgers. Not scraping by. He joined a **Neighborhood Restoration Cooperative**, rebuilding housing and walkable transit routes.

He earns **L$** based on skilled labor tiers, documented hours, and audit-aligned output.

He also receives S$ to stabilize his transition: safe housing, transit access, and Civic Tech credits to stay connected.

No forms. No patronizing classes on "personal responsibility." Just access, work, and structure.

III. Civic Defense Never Ends

If Andre's parole officer abuses power (or if a future charge appears) he's not alone.

Under Civic Law, all coercive interactions with the state trigger **automatic Civic Defense Facilitator assignment**. No public defender roulette. No plea deals behind closed doors.

His rights are interpreted in plain language. His Civic Facilitator reviews every form, records every interaction, and logs all process moves in public-access ledger space.

The system doesn't assume guilt. It assumes scrutiny.

IV. Accountability Isn't Conditional

Andre knows if he harms someone again, the ledger will reflect it. His Standing will drop. Consequences will activate.

But those consequences are clear, proportional, and reviewable. No hidden judges. No predatory fines. Just structural friction aligned with behavior.

He doesn't live in fear anymore.

He lives in structure.

CHAPTER 10: LIFE UNDER THE NEW CONSTITUTION — *THE FORMER CEO*

Miriam used to run a logistics firm that spanned three continents. Private equity. Offshore warehousing. Lobbyist dinners and tax gymnastics. She made $28 million the year before the collapse.

Now she makes about 9× the National Civic Median Income.

She's fine.

I. Wealth Isn't Power Anymore

Miriam didn't lose everything. But she lost untouchability.

Under Civic Law, all legacy wealth over the **10× NCMI threshold** expired unless actively reinvested into Tier I or Tier II public provisioning.

She had a choice:

- Let it decay and walk away with dignity
- Reinvest it into civic infrastructure and receive **Founding Contributor** status (non-heritable, non-legislative)

She chose the second. Not for control. For relevance.

II. No More Ownership Without Labor

Her former company is now a **Decentralized Logistics Cooperative**, managed by regional panels and audited Civic Supply Chains.

She doesn't own it. She works for it.

Miriam now holds a **Level III Strategic Logistics License**, granted through a national skills and ethics assessment.

She designs routing systems, negotiates border corridor contracts, and earns **E$** and **L$** based on measurable logistical impact, not shareholder return.

She still wears suits. But she doesn't write her own salary anymore.

III. Civic Panels > Private Boards

Once a month, Miriam sits on a Civic Enterprise Panel. She reviews proposals from small distribution startups, assesses audit failures, and debates labor automation thresholds.

Her voice matters. But it's one voice of many.

She was chosen by lot, not résumé. She gets rotated off after 6 months. No reappointment. No insider pool. No backchannel.

Her influence is temporary. Her responsibility is constant.

IV. What Legacy Really Means

Her children didn't inherit her portfolio. There's no estate tax because there's no estate accumulation.

What they inherit instead:

- Her verified Civic Standing
- Her public contributions ledger
- Her recorded mentorship hours (which convert into Civic Learning Credits for the recipients)

Miriam isn't bitter. She's relieved.

No lawsuits. No parasitic heirs. No illusion of empire. Just clarity.

And for the first time in decades, her work builds something permanent.

CHAPTER 11: LIFE UNDER THE NEW CONSTITUTION — *THE TEEN VOTER*

Nia voted for the first time at sixteen.

Not in a mock election. Not for class president. For a real civic panel seat that would help decide local provisioning for housing and food distribution in her district.

She wasn't nervous. She was ready. Because she'd been training for this since she was twelve.

I. Civics Is a System, Not a Slogan

Under the Civic Constitution, all students between 12–17 participate in a **Civic Readiness Track** as part of their public learning.

No grades. No standardized tests. Just:

- Participatory simulations (panel votes, conflict mediation)
- Roleplay of historical events and economic scenarios
- Live Q&A sessions with local facilitators and panelists
- Skill badges earned through practical knowledge (labor law, audit ethics, resource flows)

By sixteen, Nia knew:

- How the Civic Dollar economy worked
- How Enterprise proposals were structured
- How audit and Standing systems prevented capture

So when she got her first ballot, it wasn't a mystery. It was muscle memory.

II. Voting That Actually Counts

Her ballot wasn't performative. She didn't vote for a person with a slogan.

She voted in three domains:

1. **Local provisioning tiers** (how surplus S$ should be allocated)
2. **Panelist elections** (choosing who would sit on the next Civic Resolution Board)
3. **Amendment Feedback** (confirming or contesting a proposed change to a regional scheduling policy)

Each vote was backed by ledger summaries, proposal breakdowns, and a visual logic chain she'd been taught to parse.

She clicked "submit." Her vote logged instantly. The ledger updated in real time.

She didn't wonder if it got counted. She could see it.

III. Participation Isn't Optional, But It's Not a Chore

Nia is required to vote. Every eligible citizen is. Civic Standing depends on it.

But she doesn't dread it. Because her first vote wasn't just about policy. It was about **belonging**.

The Civic Constitution doesn't treat youth as cargo. It treats them as pre-citizens, people in training to hold weight.

She holds it now. And she knows exactly how much it matters.

CHAPTER 12: LIFE UNDER THE NEW CONSTITUTION — *THE CIVIC PANELIST*

Carlos never ran for office. He didn't donate to campaigns. He'd never even spoken at a town hall.

But last Tuesday, he helped write a law.

Not as a protester. Not as a petitioner. As a **Civic Panelist:** one of fifteen randomly selected citizens seated on a National Labor Protocol Panel.

He's a forklift operator. No law degree. No blue check. Just a citizen with Standing.

I. Selection by Lot, Not Ladder

Under the Civic Constitution, all major proposals that affect provisioning, structure, or labor rights must pass through **Deliberative Civic Panels**.

The members are chosen randomly from eligible citizens with:

- A verified Civic Standing above the minimum threshold
- No active conflicts of interest
- Demonstrated contribution history (labor, care, or service)

Carlos got a notice via Civic CommsNet. It included:

- The panel topic (Enterprise Contract Disqualification Reform)
- Time commitment (20 hours across two weeks)
- Compensation (provisioned + bonus L$)

- Access to a Civic Research Assistant and AI summarizer

He accepted.

II. Structured Deliberation, Not Debate Theater

The first session wasn't a shouting match. It was a framework.

Carlos and 14 others received:

- A summary of the current labor disqualification law
- Data on abuse patterns and failure outcomes
- Case studies from all income tiers
- Simulations showing consequences of possible changes

There were no speeches. No political parties. No one got points for posturing.

Each panelist:

- Logged questions
- Ranked priorities
- Proposed amendments in plain language

The system tracked consensus zones and flagged contested items for extended review.

III. Advisors, Not Influencers

Carlos didn't have to know everything. The system assumes citizens are intelligent but not experts.

Each panel had access to:

- Nonpartisan legal interpreters

- Conflict mediators
- Data analysts
- Ethics monitors

No one could dominate. No one could buy votes. Everything was logged and publicly auditable.

Carlos asked a question about standing restoration after labor violation appeals. He got a one-minute answer and a one-page breakdown. No jargon. No spin.

He understood it. And he voted accordingly.

IV. Law by Ledger

The final proposal had to pass with:

- 10/15 panelist approval
- Public comment quorum (auto-notified to all citizens via CivicNet)
- Compatibility review against the Civic Constitution and existing Acts

Once passed, it entered provisional force. A follow-up audit is automatically scheduled 6 months later to verify real-world impact.

If metrics show harm or deviation, it auto-triggers amendment review.

Carlos didn't just make a law.

He helped build a system that can *unmake* a bad one.

CHAPTER 13: ANTICIPATED QUESTIONS AND CRITICISMS

This isn't a utopia. It's a system.

And any system designed for 330 million people will generate confusion, resistance, and questions, especially from those raised inside legacy institutions.

What follows are some of the most common objections, misunderstandings, and critiques, answered without spin, without apologies, and without pretending every answer will satisfy everyone.

Q: What prevents this from being overthrown by elites?

A:
Nothing guarantees it won't be. That's the point.

This constitution doesn't rely on eternal virtue. It relies on structural friction:

- There's no centralized authority to capture
- Wealth cannot accumulate beyond fixed caps
- Civic Ledgers expose all major contracts, holdings, and behaviors
- Elite sabotage automatically triggers panel review, Standing drops, and public exposure

Overthrow requires coordination and opacity. This framework kills both.

Q: Isn't this just communism?

A:

No. It's not communism. It's not capitalism. It's not feudalism with better PR.

This system:

- Preserves private decision-making and small enterprise
- Assigns value to labor, not ideology
- Doesn't abolish markets, but limits hoarding and rent-seeking
- Ties income to verifiable contribution, not speculative ownership

You keep what you contribute. You lose what you try to hoard. That's not Marx. It's modern civic accounting.

Q: What if people just stop working?

A:

Then the system slows down. Services degrade. Their Civic Standing decays. Their influence disappears.

No one is forced to work but everyone is subject to consequence. Provisioning covers basic needs, not luxuries. Full access requires visible contribution.

And because the system doesn't funnel wealth upward, it creates fewer pointless jobs and more socially necessary ones. Most people want to matter. This system gives them a structured way to do that.

Q: What if people refuse to participate in panels or reviews?
A:
Then they lose participation rights. Just like skipping jury duty or tax fraud now.

The Civic system depends on *rotation, not election.* That means widespread, shared responsibility.

Panel duty is provisioned and short-term. If someone refuses, it's noted in their Standing ledger and affects future access to enterprise opportunities or regional privileges.

It's not punishment. It's consequence. A system built on rights must be built on duties too.

Q: Isn't this system vulnerable to apathy or decay over time?
A:
Yes. All systems are.

But this one has built-in self-auditing. Every policy has scheduled follow-up audits. Every citizen has visibility into core ledgers. Every allocation triggers a public trace.

Decay happens when no one notices. Here, decay is visible and it's early, often, and correctable.

Q: What if someone wants to opt out entirely?
A:
They can. No one is forced to participate. But opting out means:

- No access to Civic provisioning
- No labor contracts
- No Standing, no vote, no panel eligibility

They are not criminalized. They are not chased. They simply live outside the system. They can return any time by aligning to the same standards as everyone else.

GOVERNANCE + STRUCTURE

Q: How do we prevent bad laws from accumulating?
A:
Every law passed has:

- A built-in **sunset audit** after 6–12 months
- A **ledger-based feedback loop** that tracks real-world outcomes
- A civic panel with standing authority to amend, pause, or repeal

If a law underperforms or causes harm, it doesn't linger. It auto-triggers review. Laws must justify their continued existence.

Q: What happens if someone corrupts the ledgers?
A:
Every Civic Ledger is:

- Publicly mirrored across redundant regional nodes
- Cryptographically verified and backed by multi-panel consensus before writing
- Audited by standing Civic Transparency Boards with no overlapping appointments

Tampering one node doesn't rewrite the others. Fraud is immediately traceable.

RIGHTS + SECURITY

Q: Can the government take my stuff without due process?

A:
No. Asset redistribution or Standing reduction requires:

- Panel review with 3+ independent signatories
- Ledger-backed documentation of cause (fraud, sabotage, harm)
- Public notice and structured appeal windows

This system doesn't disappear people or property. Every coercive act is logged and reversible if wrongful.

Q: What protections exist for minorities or dissenters?

A:
This constitution guarantees:

- Civic Defense access for anyone under coercive threat
- Automatic audit triggers if Standing drops too fast or outside defined criteria
- Cultural Continuity rights (Article I, Act XXII) that cannot be revoked by panels

Dissent is ledgered, not silenced. If you speak truth, your Standing holds. If you harm others under cover of dissent, it drops.

LABOR + VALUE

Q: What happens to luxury jobs like fashion designers or video game streamers?

A:
All labor is value-ranked by Civic Panels and public demand.

- A game streamer with high engagement and civic impact (e.g., educational value, community health) earns L$
- A luxury designer creating durable, ethically sourced goods may earn E$

There's no cap on creativity. There's just a demand that value flow both ways: from labor *to* society not just labor *from* it.

Q: Can I still run my own business?

A:
Yes, if it aligns with Civic ethics and ledger visibility.

You don't "own" it in the old way. You **steward** it:

- Transparent input/output flows
- Fair labor contracts
- Value reinvestment over extraction

Profit exists. Predation doesn't.

TRANSITION + CONTINUITY

Q: What happens to disabled people or those who can't work?

A:
They are fully provisioned.

- Caregiving (received or given) is ledgered labor
- Inability to work does not affect S$ access
- Dignity Zones ensure housing, medical access, and community autonomy

The system honors need without means-testing cruelty.

Q: Is this all just too complex to work?

A:
Only if you try to run it with paper.

This system relies on:

- Ledger automation
- Civic AI filters
- Real-time data transparency

You already trust invisible systems for banking, GPS, and elections. This just makes them honest.

AI + TECHNOLOGY

Q: Isn't this just technocracy? What about human judgment?
A:
No. AI here is a **tool**, not a ruler.

- Civic AI systems only summarize data, flag anomalies, and handle mechanical sorting
- **All decisions** (labor audits, disqualifications, proposals) require human panels
- Every AI recommendation is publicly overrideable by citizen vote or review

It's not rule *by* algorithms. It's rule *with* accountability tools.

Q: What stops AI from evolving into central control?
A:
This Constitution explicitly bans:

- Autonomous weapon control (Act XX)
- Self-modifying AI agents with authority over ledgers
- Any AI from holding civic Standing or panel eligibility

Synthetic systems are advisory only. They cannot initiate or enforce law.

IDEOLOGY + BELIEF

Q: What about religion? Can faith groups operate under this system?

A:
Yes, with boundaries.

- Faith institutions are protected under **Cultural Continuity rights**
- They can receive S$ provisioning, host services, form communities
- They cannot bypass ledger visibility, create shadow hierarchies, or extract passive income

Spiritual life is honored. Theocracy is not.

Q: What if my belief system rejects ledger tracking or participation?

A:
Then you are free to live outside the Civic system. No Standing, no panels, no provisioning but no interference either.

Your rights to privacy and separation are upheld.

But you don't get civic power from a position of nonparticipation. That's the tradeoff.

FREEDOM + AUTONOMY

Q: Isn't mandatory voting authoritarian?

A:
No more than mandatory taxes or emergency services.

Voting is:

- Short, structured, and ledgered
- Accompanied by clear summaries and feedback tools
- Penalized only through Standing decay and not jail or fines

You are required to show up. You are never required to vote a certain way.

Q: What if someone wants to live fully off-grid with no phone, no net, and no ledgers?

A:
They can. Nothing in the Constitution forces digital compliance outside of:

- Voting
- Contractual labor
- Civic access

If you want zero contact, you're free to build your own parallel life. But Civic resources will not subsidize it.

Autonomy does not mean obligation-free entitlement.

LEGACY + CULTURE

Q: What happens to art, music, and history? Does this system erase the past?

A:
No. It preserves the past **by integrating it.**

- Artists are provisioned like any other laborer based on public value and engagement
- Cultural memory is enshrined in **Acts on Indigenous Continuity, Archive Protection, and Language Stewardship**
- Legacy media is retained but its influence is openly debated, not covertly monetized

Art doesn't die. It just stops being sold back to us by corporations that didn't make it.

Q: What happens to the flag? To holidays? To national identity?

A:
Those become civic questions and not propaganda.

- New holidays may be proposed via citizen initiative
- Legacy holidays are retained or replaced based on public vote
- The flag is a visual symbol, not a sacred object

Culture is dynamic. So is identity. This system doesn't erase. It invites reinterpretation, in the open.

FINAL CHAPTER: IF YOU'RE READING THIS AFTER THE FALL

This wasn't supposed to be prophecy.

It was a map. A manual. A warning.

But if you're reading this after the systems collapsed, after the supply chains broke, after the trust dissolved, after the institutions turned inward and violent, then this isn't theory anymore. It's salvage.

I. Do Not Panic. Do Not Wait.

The old world will not come back. The ones in charge won't fix it. Their power depends on the dysfunction staying permanent.

You don't need to wait for permission. You don't need to convince them. You don't need to vote harder.

You need to act.

Now.

II. What To Do First

1. **Secure a Core Group.**
   Minimum five people. Ideally 7–13. Skills matter less than willingness to work together. Rotate facilitation. No heroes.

2. **Access or Reproduce the Civic Acts.**
   You can rebuild from fragments. Even one act (Labor, Provisioning, Panels) can anchor a region.

3. **Establish Local Ledgers.**
   Paper if necessary. Public. Open. Transparent. Who contributes, who receives, who decides.

4. **Reject All Extractors.**
   No landlords. No warlords. No corporate holdouts offering "help" in exchange for power. If it can't survive open accounting, it doesn't belong.

5. **Enforce Standing by Conduct, Not Class.**
   Your group must earn legitimacy by action, not by title or seniority. Use Standing. Revoke it when needed.

III. What To Protect

- **Civic Defense Systems**
  No one goes unrepresented. No coercive power operates without review.

- **Cultural Continuity**
  Keep memory alive. Language. Music. Ritual. These are not luxuries. They are immune defense against mental colonization.

- **Children**
  Do not draft them into labor or war. Teach them how to panel, how to audit, how to decide. They are not legacy. They are load-bearing.

- **Ledgers**
  Never let decision-making go dark. If it isn't written down and visible, it doesn't exist.

IV. What Not To Become

Don't become the last empire's reflection.

- Don't rebuild hierarchy and call it safety.
- Don't centralize force and call it order.
- Don't hoard and call it prudence.

This system was built to outlive collapse by refusing the behaviors that caused it.

Hold the line. Even when scared. Especially when scared.

V. What Happens Next

The Civic Constitution is a living tool. It won't save you, but it can *equip* you.

Use it to:

- Rebuild local trust
- Restore shared labor and shared gain
- Replace panic with structure

You're not alone. Others are out there doing the same. Form nodes. Share practices. Stay distributed.

And if you rebuild well enough, they'll call this *the second founding*.

Not of a nation.

Of a people who finally chose to grow up.

ABOUT THE AUTHOR

James "JiLm" Ergle writes for people who know something's broken and want more than slogans. He's a political essayist, cartoonist, and criminal investigator who's spent years inside the systems he now critiques.

His Substack, [Radical Leanings](), combines essays, political cartoons, and structural breakdowns for readers who want to understand how power really works and how it might be replaced. He writes like someone explaining the world to his younger self, and thousands of readers have joined him for that reason.

This is his fourth book. The L is silent. The logic is not.

www.ingramcontent.com/pod-product-compliance
Lightning Source LLC
Chambersburg PA
CBHW070613030426
42337CB00020B/3781